KU-208-722

Things to Make and Do

BY CHARLES VIVIAN

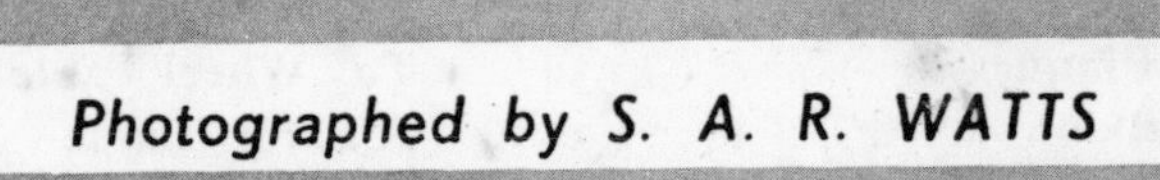

Photographed by S. A. R. WATTS

A DAILY MAIL PUBLICATION

CONTENTS

THE BALLOON AND TEACUP TRICK

You will require : *Two teacups, one strong balloon.*

SHOW your friend a balloon and two teacups on the table. Ask him if he can raise both cups from the table with the aid of the balloon.

When he has tried, and failed, show him how it is done. Hold both cups fairly close together, with the balloon between them. Now carefully blow the balloon up. (Fig. 1.)

You will discover that, when the balloon is fully inflated, both teacups will be attached to it. When the balloon is raised, both cups can be easily lifted from the table. This is because the air pressure which you have forced into the balloon has pushed the rubber wall of the balloon tightly inside the cups.

There is a final word of warning. Balloons have been known to burst. Please do not use Mother's best china-ware for the experiment ! (Fig. 2.)

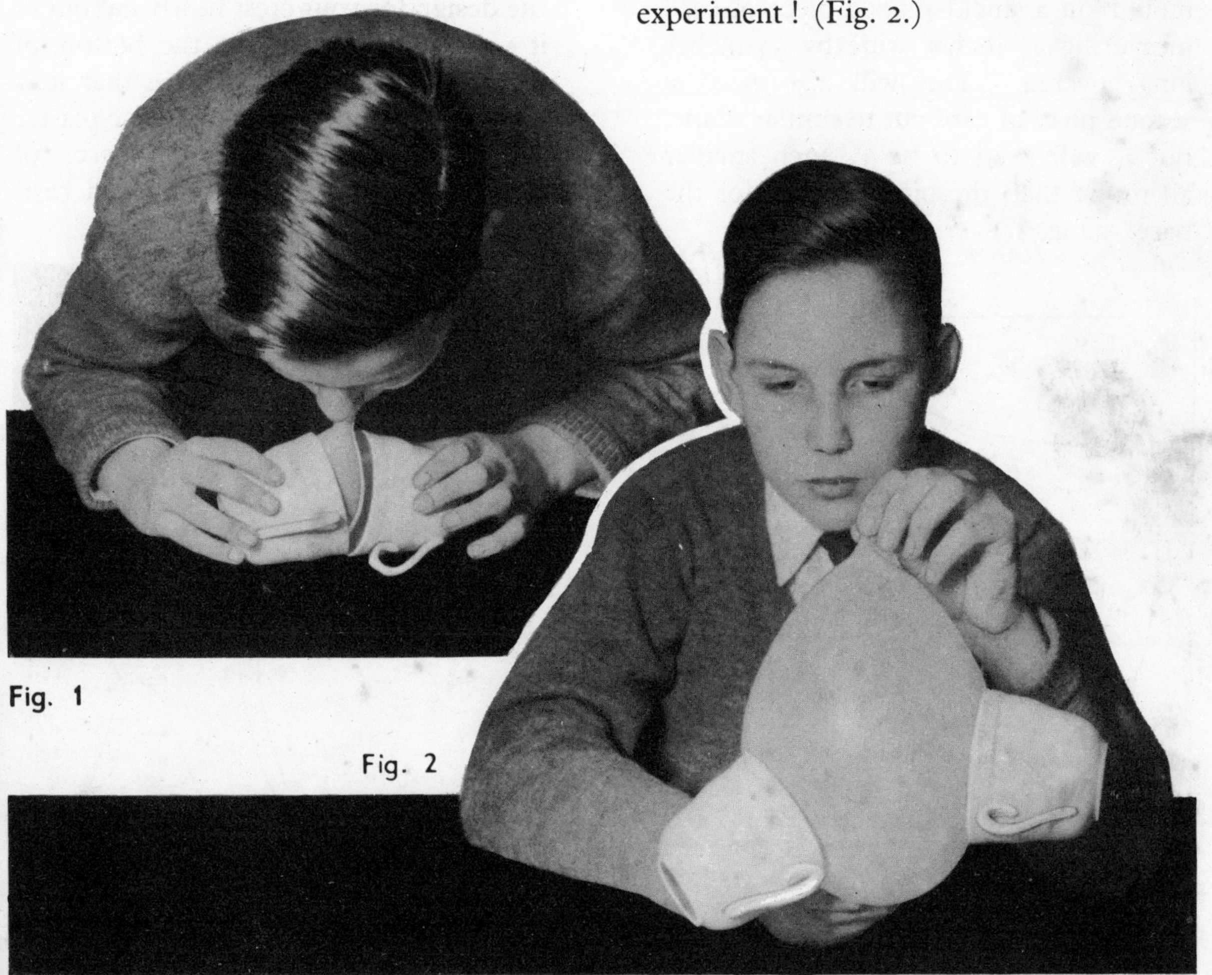

Fig. 1

Fig. 2

MAKE YOUR OWN FAMILY CRESTS

You will require: *Cardboard, pencil, scissors, water, paints, plaster of Paris, paper-clip.*

HAVE you ever thought what good fun it would be if you had a family crest? Why not try designing your own? Choose some very simple design for your first attempt. When you find out what a fascinating pastime it is you will soon be making larger and much more complicated crests.

Your first need will be a mould from which to cast your crests. The moulds can be made from thin cardboard or even thick paper, cut to the required size and shape. For the base of your mould cut a shield-shaped piece of card measuring $4\frac{1}{2}$ inches wide by $5\frac{1}{2}$ inches long, overall. You will also need a second piece of card cut to similar shape, but it will need to be $\frac{1}{16}$ inch smaller all round than the piece of card for the base. (Fig. 1.)

Now cut a long strip of thin card about 2 inches wide. Fold this in half down the centre. Cut triangular-shaped tabs on one edge of the strip. Bend and gum the tabs under the cardboard base so that the remainer of the strip forms a wall for your mould. When this wall is in position, hold the mould up to the light. If you can see any pinholes of light, where the wall joins the base, seal them from the outside with pieces of newspaper gummed into appropriate positions. (Fig. 2.)

The second piece of cardboard—with the design for your crest neatly cut out of it—is now gummed into the bottom of the mould. Make quite sure that it is securely gummed down, otherwise plaster may flow between the two pieces of cardboard and spoil your finished cast. (Fig. 3.)

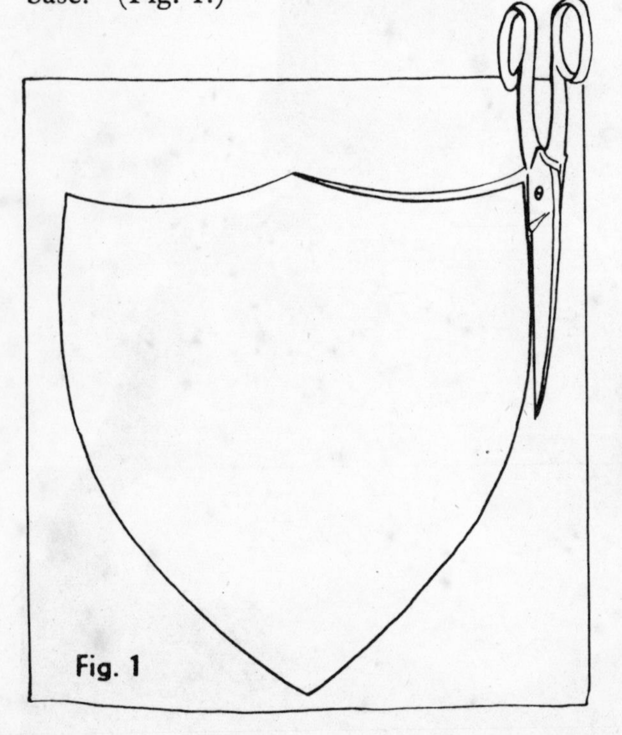

Fig. 1

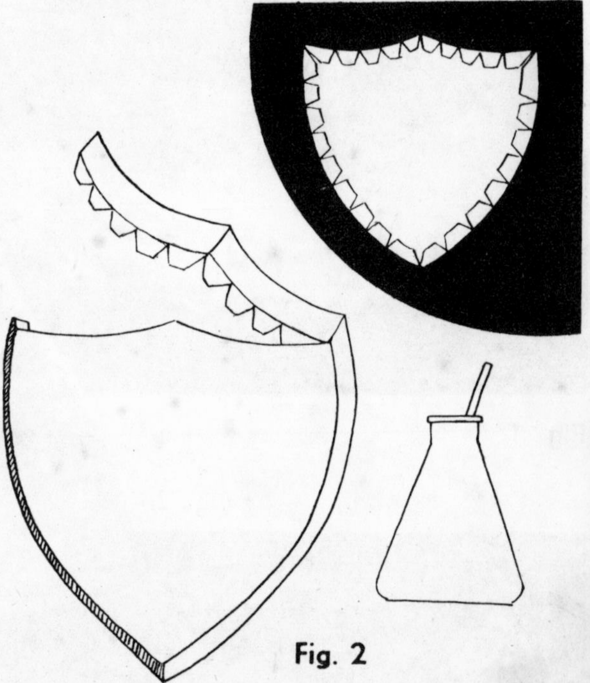

Fig. 2

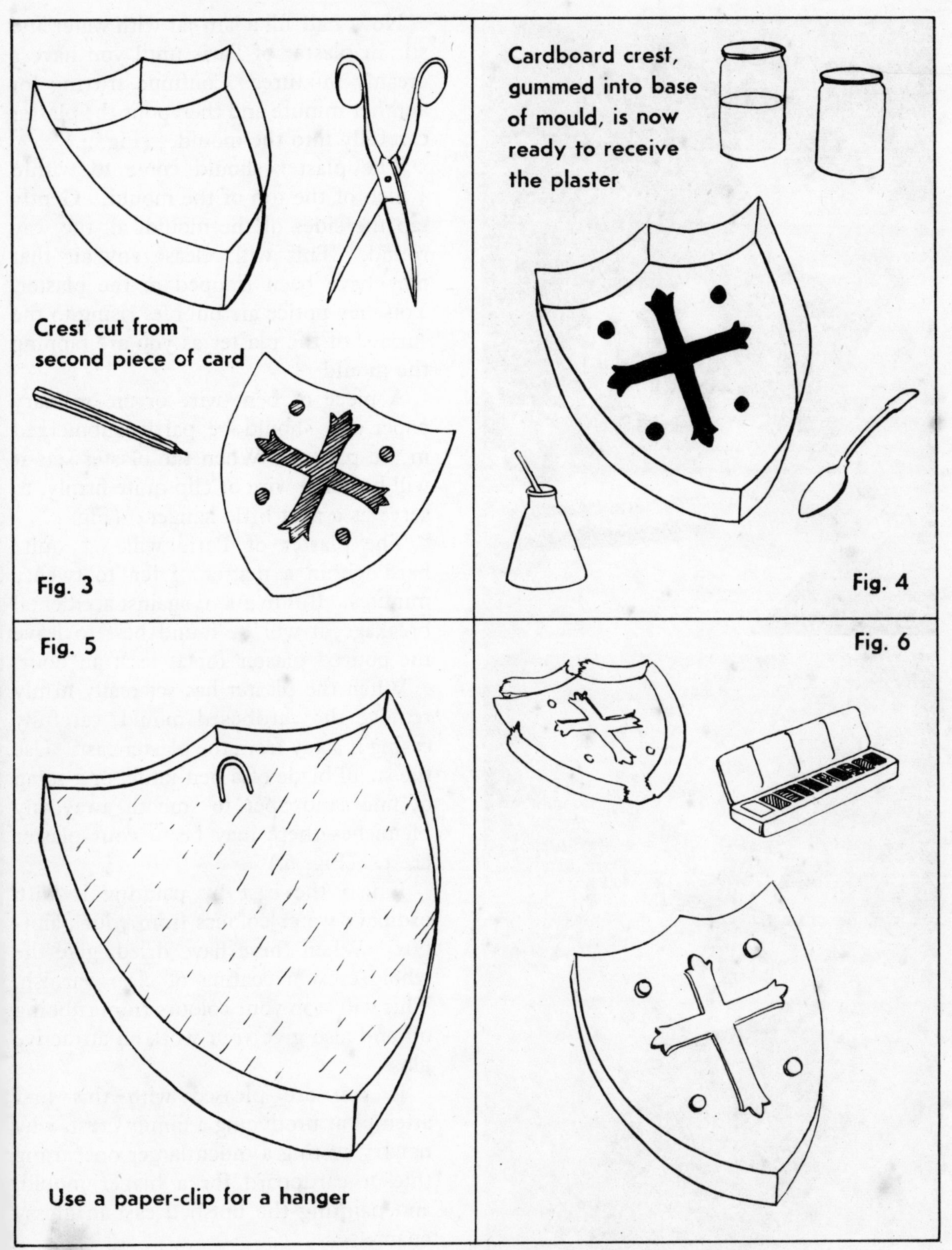
Crest cut from
second piece of card
Fig. 3
Cardboard crest,
gummed into base
of mould, is now
ready to receive
the plaster
Fig. 4
Fig. 5
Use a paper-clip for a hanger
Fig. 6

Now, half fill a jam-jar with water and stir in plaster of Paris until you have a creamy mixture. Continue stirring for another minute and then pour the plaster carefully into the mould. (Fig. 4.)

The plaster should come to within $\frac{1}{4}$ inch of the top of the mould. Gently tap the sides of the mould, all the way round. This will release any air that may have been trapped in the plaster. You may notice air bubbles rising to the surface of the plaster as you are tapping the mould.

A piece of bent wire or an ordinary paper-clip should be partly submerged in the plaster. When the plaster sets it will hold the wire or clip quite firmly, to serve as a neat little hanger. (Fig. 5.)

The plaster of Paris will set quite hard within a matter of ten to twenty minutes. But to guard against accidental breakage, it will be found best to leave the poured plaster for at least an hour.

When the plaster has set really firmly remove the cardboard mould, carefully easing it away from the plaster cast. Use the small blade of a pen-knife, or a scrap of fine sandpaper to smooth away any blemishes there may be in your plaster crest. (Fig. 6.)

Finish the cast by painting it with ordinary water colours from your paint-box. When these have dried, give the whole crest a coating of clear varnish. This will stop your colours from rubbing off and also give your work an attractive gloss.

If you are pleased with this first attempt at producing a family crest, why not try casting a much larger one, using thicker cardboard for a bigger mould, and painting the finished cast in glossy enamels?

THE OBEDIENT SIXPENCE

You will require : *Tumbler, two pennies, sixpence.*

SUPPORT an upturned tumbler on two pennies, with a sixpence between them. The simple diagram in Fig. 1 shows how the coins are placed in relation to the tumbler.

The trick is to extract the sixpence from under the tumbler without touching either the pennies, the tumbler—or the sixpence!

Impossible, you say? That's just what Pauline thought. So along comes Robert to show her how it is done.

To Pauline's surprise all he did was to scratch with his forefinger at the tablecloth, immediately in front of the tumbler. As Robert performed this simple operation the sixpence gradually moved out from under the tumbler until it was quite clear of the glass. (Fig. 2.)

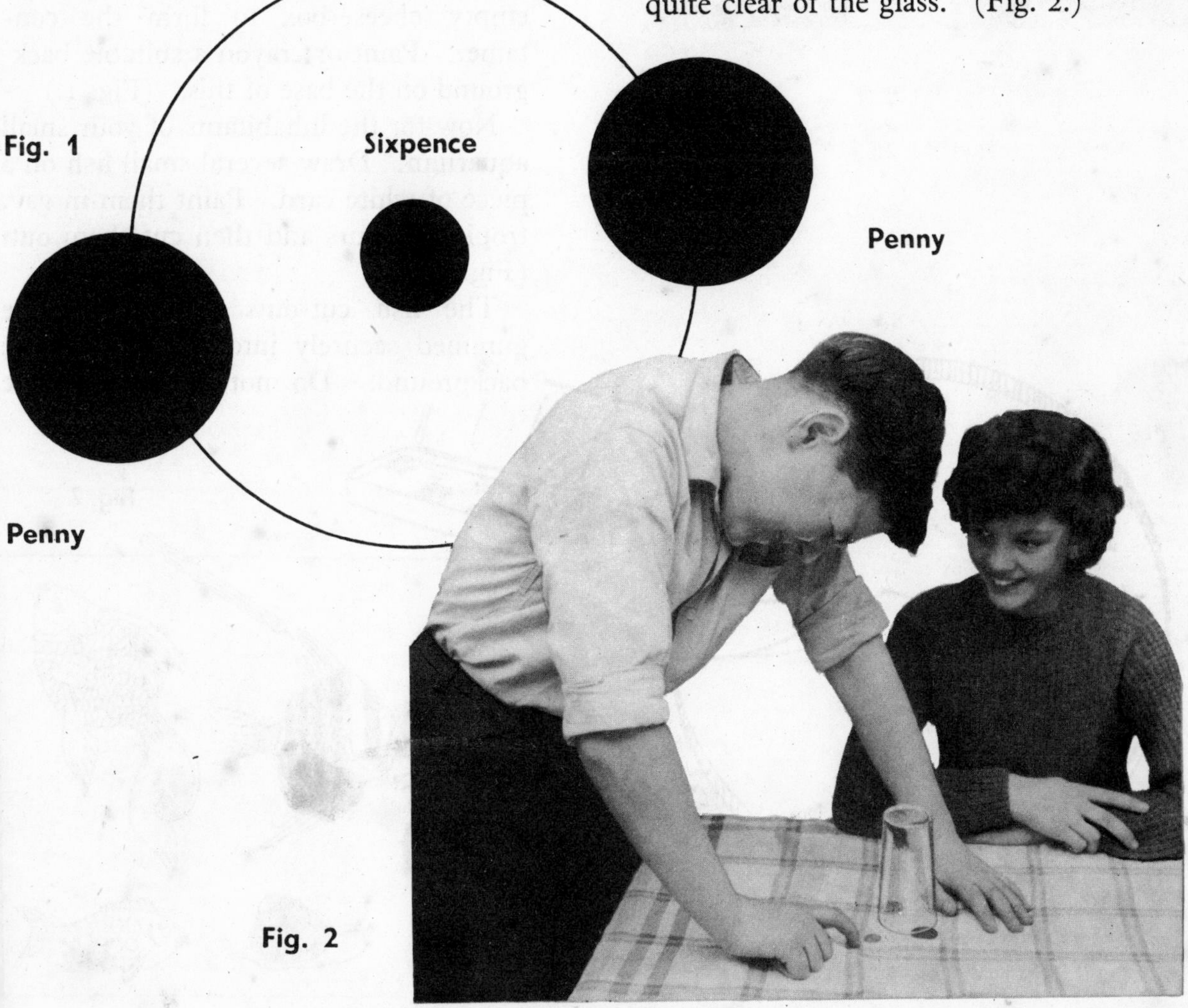

Fig. 1

Fig. 2

CHEESE-BOX AQUARIUMS

You will require: *A cheese-box, card-board, gum, paints, pencil, scissors, cellophane, and an elastic band.*

EVER been heart-broken over a pet goldfish that has died? Ever thought it rather a fag to keep changing the water in your aquarium? Ever been afraid that the cat would have a fishy snack while you were not looking? Yes! Then what you need is a trouble-free cheese-box aquarium. Have all the colourful delights of an aquarium, with none of the chores!

Use the bottom or lid of a round, empty cheese-box to form the container. Paint or crayon a suitable background on the base of this. (Fig. 1.)

Now for the inhabitants of your small aquarium. Draw several small fish on a piece of white card. Paint them in gay, tropical colours and then cut them out. (Fig. 2.)

The fish cut-outs should now be gummed securely into position on the background. Do not overstock these

Fig. 1

Fig. 2

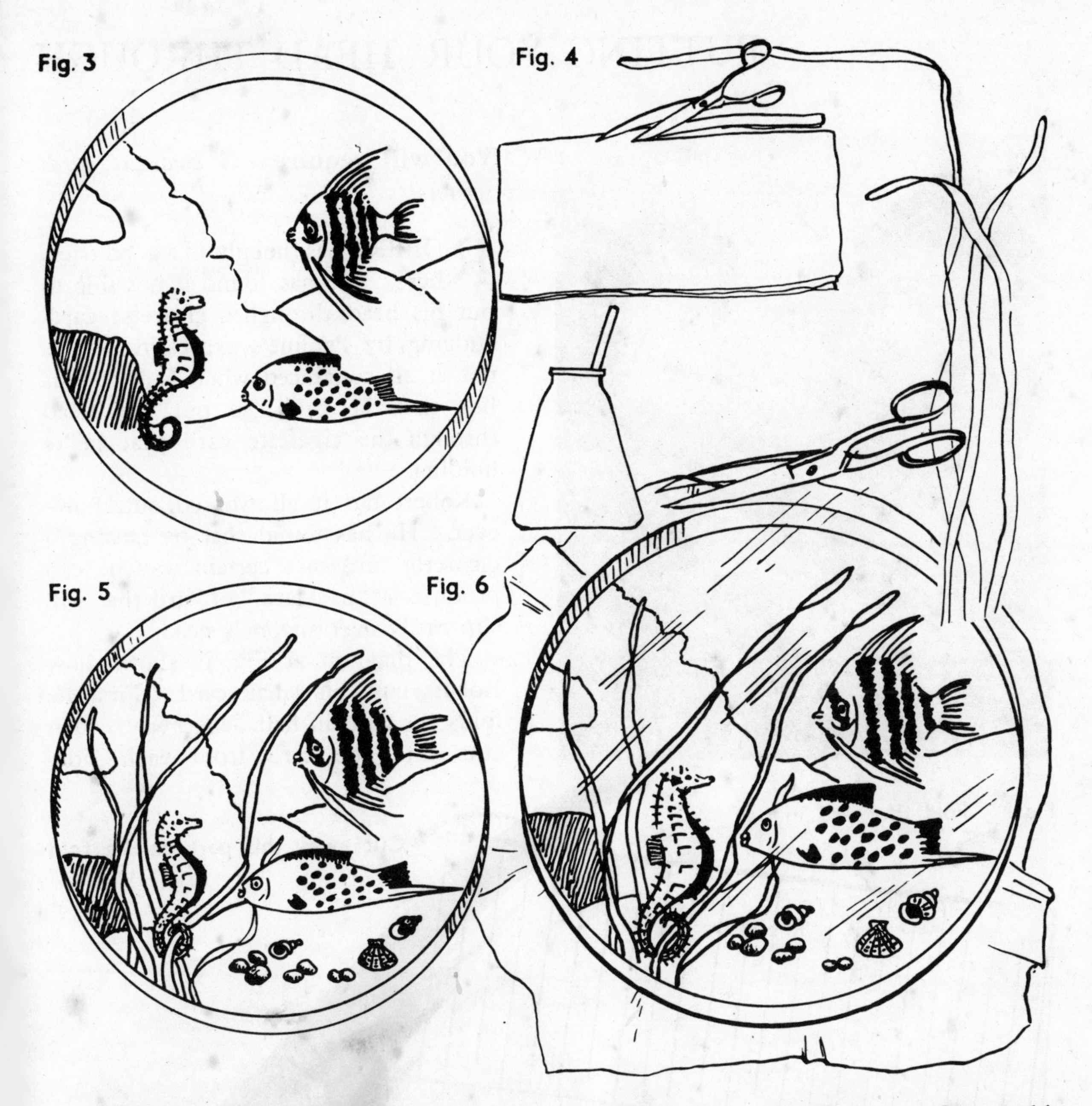

small aquariums. Two or three fish are enough. (Fig. 3.)

Thin strands of weed can be cut from paper and then suitably coloured. (Fig. 4.)

When the weed has been tastefully arranged, gum a few small shells and stones on the bed of your aquarium. (Fig. 5.)

Cover the finished little aquarium with a sheet of cellophane. Secure this to the sides of the box with a strong elastic band. Pass a damp sponge over the front of the cellophane. This will make it shrink slightly and help to remove any creases that may have occurred. Use scissors to cut off surplus cellophane beyond the elastic band. (Fig. 6.)

PUTTING YOUR HEAD THROUGH

You will require: *A cigarette card, scissors.*

ROBERT has thought of a good trick, here. He has found it possible to put his head through a cigarette card. Judging by Pauline's expression she is not at all convinced when Robert tells her that he can also put her head through the cigarette card that he is holding.

Robert has it all worked out, however. He has found that by cutting a cigarette card in a certain way he can produce a " necklace " of card that will slip easily over anyone's head.

The diagram at Fig. 1 shows how Robert cuts his small card. First he folds the card in half, lengthways, then cuts into the card from each side.

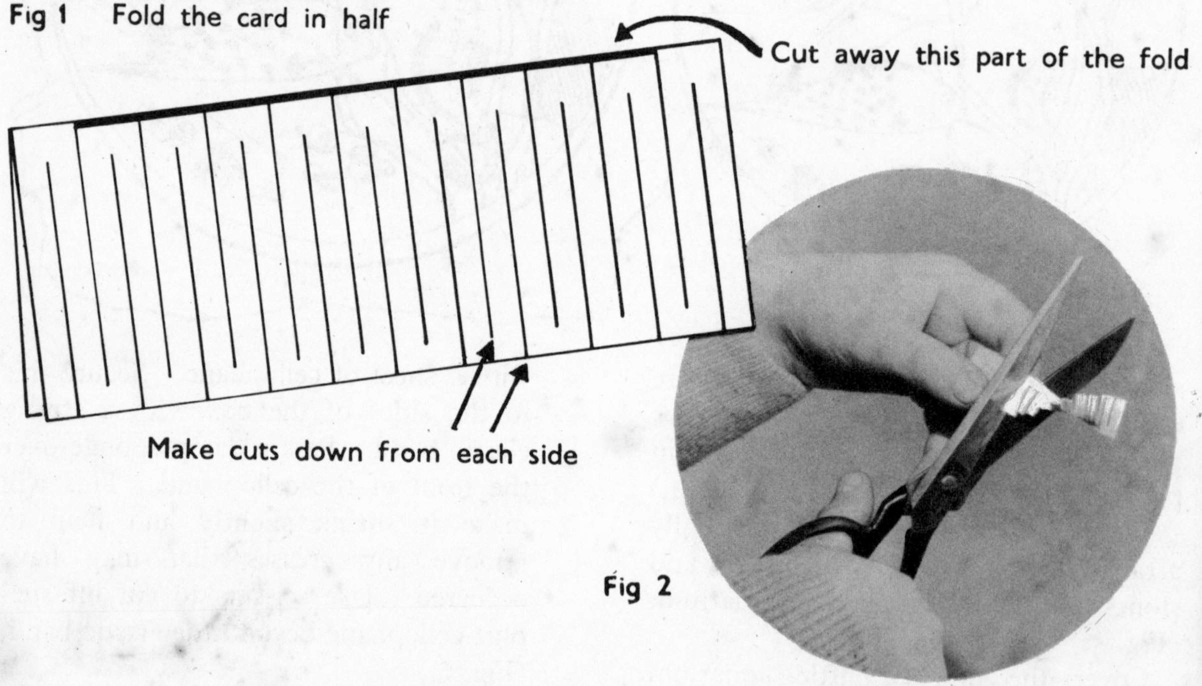

A CIGARETTE CARD

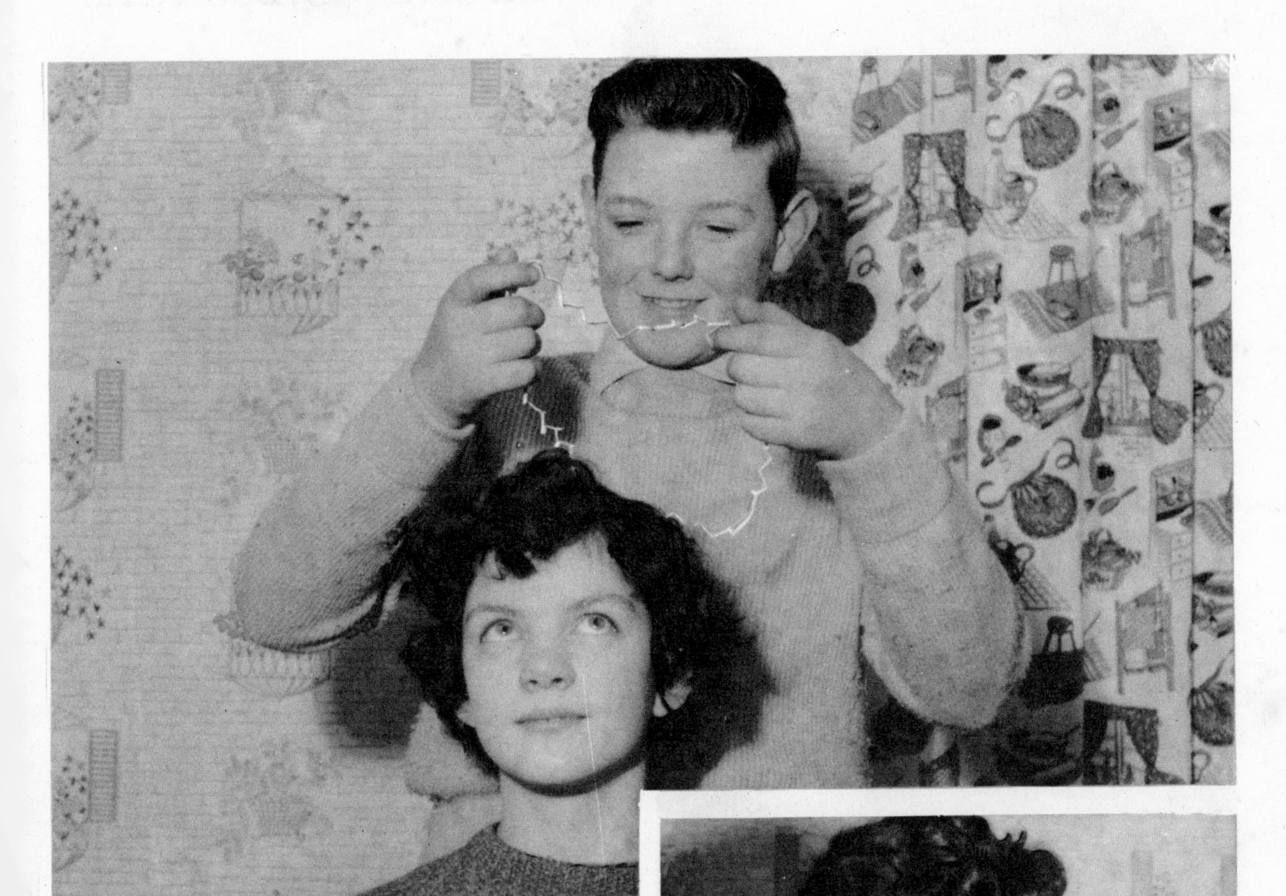

Notice that he does not let the cuts meet. Also, when all the cuts have been made, he snips off the folds from all except the extreme ends of the card. Fig. 2 shows the care with which he handles the scissors when cutting the small card.

Once the card has been cut, Robert carefully unfolds it until he has a large circle of card. He really enjoys placing this over Pauline's head.

As you can see (right), Pauline is really surprised to find that Robert has actually succeeded in putting her head through that small cigarette card.

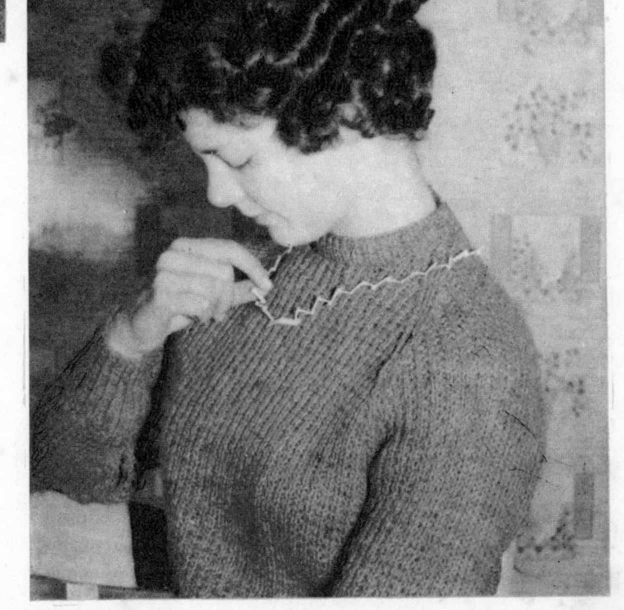

HOW TO SEND SECRET MESSAGES

You will require : *A lemon, small jar, knife, juice extractor, pen-holder, new nib, drawing-paper, candle and matches.*

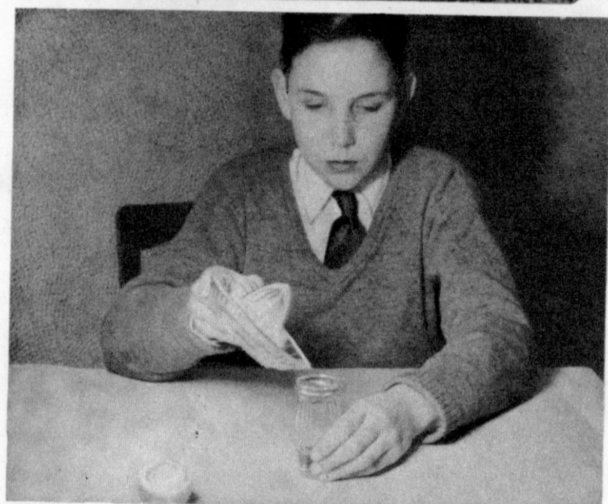

HERE is a chance to send your friends secret messages, written in invisible ink. Just think what fun it will be, with other people passing on what they think is a blank sheet of paper, and only your friend knowing that it contains a secret letter from you.

Your invisible ink consists of the juice of a lemon. This is best kept in a small, clean jar. An empty fish-paste-jar makes a suitable inkwell.

It is important that you use either a new nib, or at least one which you have thoroughly cleaned, when writing your secret messages. If possible, use thick white drawing-paper on which to write.

Once the lemon juice has dried it will be hard to find any trace of a message on the paper. But all that your friend has to do, is to hold the paper close to a candle or similar small flame. The lemon juice combines with oxygen when heated, and forms dark brown characters on the white paper.

THE THIRSTY JAM-JAR

You will require : *A coin, a saucer, a stub of candle, a jam-jar, water, and matches.*

HERE is another trick where air pressure will help you to mystify your friends. First, pour a little water into a saucer and then place a small coin below the level of the water to one side of the saucer. Can your friend, with the help of the candle and the jam-jar, remove the water, thus leaving the coin high and dry? Tell him that on no account is he allowed to touch or tilt the saucer. Instead, to help him, you have provided an extremely thirsty jam-jar.

Has he given up yet? When he does, light the stub of candle and stand it in the centre of the saucer. Now carefully place the upturned jar over the candle.

Within seconds, the thirsty jam-jar will have greedily swallowed all the water leaving the coin uncovered. What really happens? The flame of the candle consumes all the oxygen from the air trapped in the jar. This is about one-fifth of the jar's content of air. Outer air pressure dislikes even a partial vacuum of this nature, and promptly presses down on the surface of the water in the saucer with sufficient force to drive it up into the jar.

HOME-MADE MUSIC

You will require : *Comb, tissue-paper, empty bottles, water, spoons.*

EVER had a strong desire to make music, with no musical instruments to hand ? Robert and Terry had just that desire the other day.

Robert cut a square of thin tissue-paper and wrapped this around a comb. By placing this to his lips and humming through it he produced a nice " jazzy " sound.

Young Terry was a little more ambitious. He decided to make himself a xylophone. He rummaged around the cupboards at home until he had unearthed eight empty bottles, all more or less the same size.

He carefully put water into each of the bottles, adding more water to each successive bottle so that, while the first bottle had scarcely any water in it, the last was almost full.

When Terry struck the various bottles with a spoon, he found that each produced its own distinctive note. By adding a little water here and removing a little water there, he was finally able to produce quite a fair octave of notes. Here you can see Robert and Terry really getting into the swing of it. Later, Robert took over the xylophone while Terry got busy with comb and paper. Robert had been itching to get at those bottles ever since Terry had filled them. He found that by using forks instead of spoons he could produce some really sparkling notes from those bottles.

GETTING A QUART IN A PINT POT

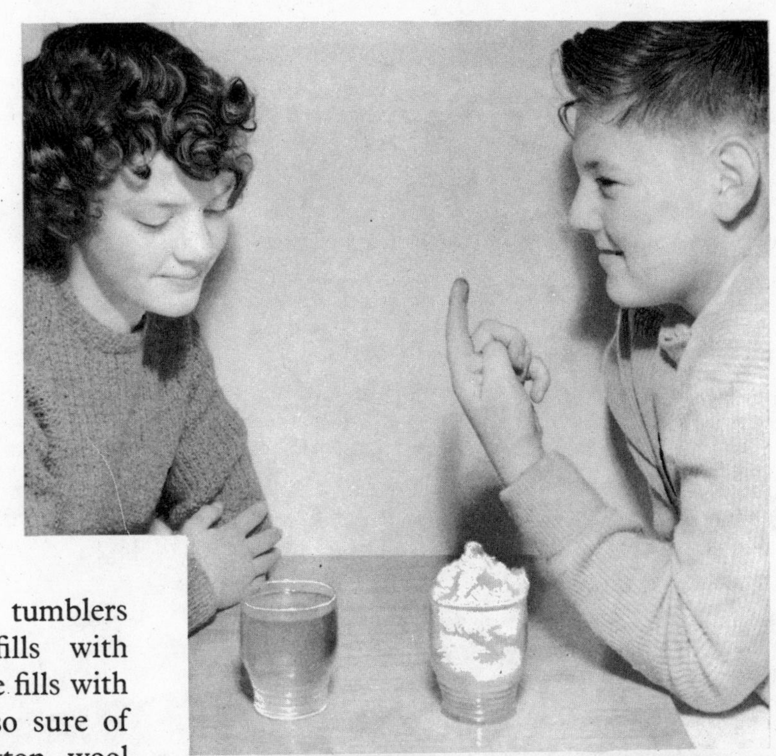

You will require: *Two tumblers, cotton wool, water.*

ROBERT has another trick here with which to mystify Pauline. He has been talking a lot about being able to get a quart into a pint pot. Pauline has already told him that she thinks it quite impossible.

Robert now produces two tumblers of equal size. One he fills with water. The second tumbler he fills with cotton wool. In fact, he is so sure of himself that he has the cotton wool sticking up well above the edge of the tumbler.

He tells Pauline that he can easily get both the water and the cotton wool in *one* tumbler, without spilling a drop of water.

To Pauline's surprise, he easily accomplishes this. She thought he would have some trick to explain the whole thing away. Instead, Robert simply empties the tumbler of water into the tumbler containing the cotton wool. The single tumbler contains both the water and the wool.

The wool is so absorbent that it soaks up all the water and adds hardly any additional bulk.

A PUPPET THEATRE

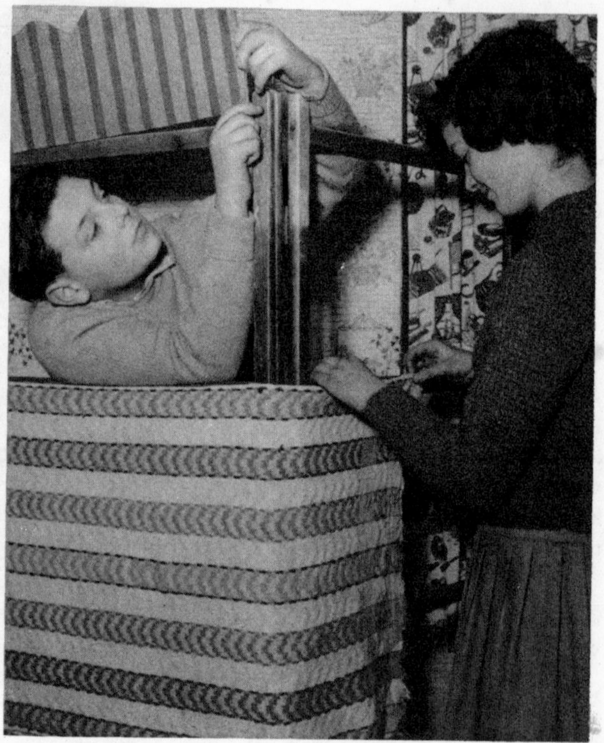

You will require : *Clothes-horse, cardboard, scissors, brush and paints, drawing-pins, towels.*

WHENEVER there is a party in the offing—or even just a gathering of your friends—it is a good idea to surprise your visitors with a puppet show.

You will probably think that the most difficult part will be the construction of a suitable theatre from which to give your shows. This will prove an easy matter, providing you can find or borrow an old clothes-horse for the occasion.

Measure the top of the centre partition of the clothes-horse and cut a piece of strong cardboard to this length by some ten inches in width. Cut the top of this piece of cardboard to an attractively decorated shape, and then paint the front of it in gay stripes.

Use drawing-pins to hold the cardboard strip in position on top of the clothes-horse. Now cover all but the proscenium of your puppet theatre with blankets, sheets or, better still, gaily striped towels, neatly pinned into position. Your home-made theatre will then be ready for its first show.

HAND PUPPETS

You will require : *Brush and paints, pair of hands.*

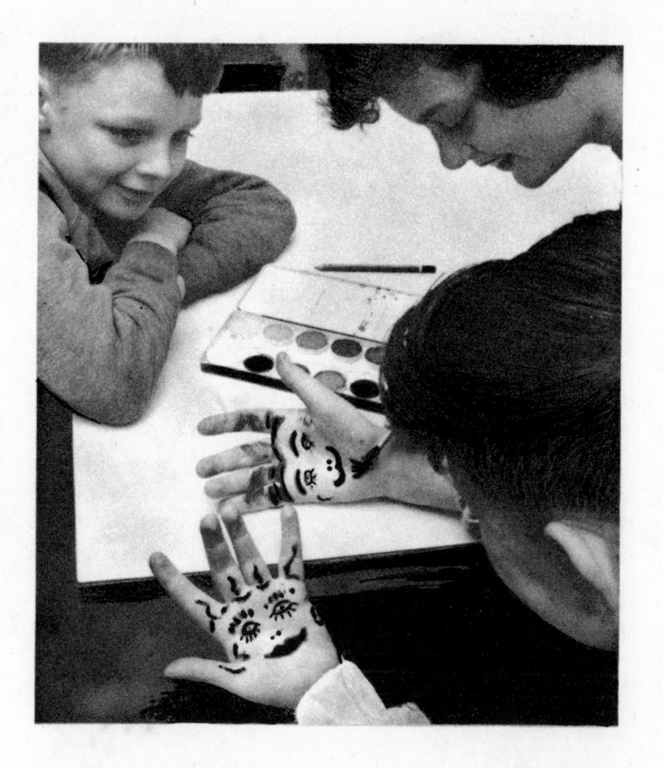

POSSIBLY the easiest and quickest way of making puppets for your home-made theatre is to use your own hands for the heads of the characters in your play.

You will find it great fun painting faces on the palms of your hands. You will be able to paint one hand yourself, but will probably find it best to enlist the aid of a friend in painting your second palm. The brush tickles a little, I am afraid, but providing you use ordinary water colours from your paint-box you will have no difficulty in getting your hands clean again by washing with ordinary soap and water. The picture shows Pauline completing a " merry twosome " on Robert's right hand.

Collars and scarves of paper can be tied or secured with elastic bands around the wrists. The performer then sits or kneels comfortably on a cushion behind the clothes-horse, and raises his arms just high enough to allow his hands and wrists to appear in the proscenium of the puppet theatre.

In practice, it will be found that by opening and closing the palms of the hands it will be possible to provide your small characters with different expressions—to make them appear to talk, to wink, etc.

AN AIR-PRESSURE EXPERIMENT

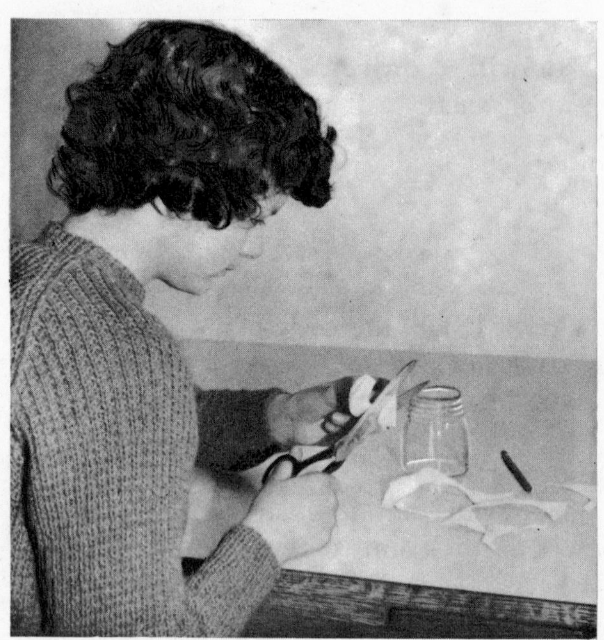

You will require : *Two tumblers, pencil, scissors, blotting-paper, water, matches.*

HERE is a simple experiment which clearly demonstrates the force of the air-pressure which surrounds us.

Place an upturned tumbler on a double thickness of blotting-paper and draw round it with a soft-lead pencil.

Cut the circles of blotting-paper out, fold them in half and then remove a circular portion from the centre. This will leave you with two rings of blotting-paper, about three-quarters of an inch wide all round.

Lightly crumple some of the odd pieces of blotting-paper and drop them into one of the tumblers. Now soak the two rings of blotting-paper in a saucer of water for a few moments.

The damp rings of blotting-paper are placed on top of the tumbler which holds the crumpled pieces of paper. Light a match and drop it on top of the crumpled blotting-paper in the bottom of the tumbler.

When the blotting-paper has caught alight, place the second tumbler, upturned, on top of the first. Press down firmly on to the paper rings until the flame in the tumblers has died out.

Now lift the top tumbler. If your experiment has been successful you will find that both tumblers appear to be glued together. The flame in the tumblers has used up all the oxygen. The outer air tries to rush into this partial vacuum, but the damp rings of blotting-paper make an air-tight seal. The air presses so strongly against the outer surfaces of the tumblers that it makes them appear to be glued together.

If you take both tumblers in your hands and pull them apart, you will hear a mild explosion as the outer air rushes in.

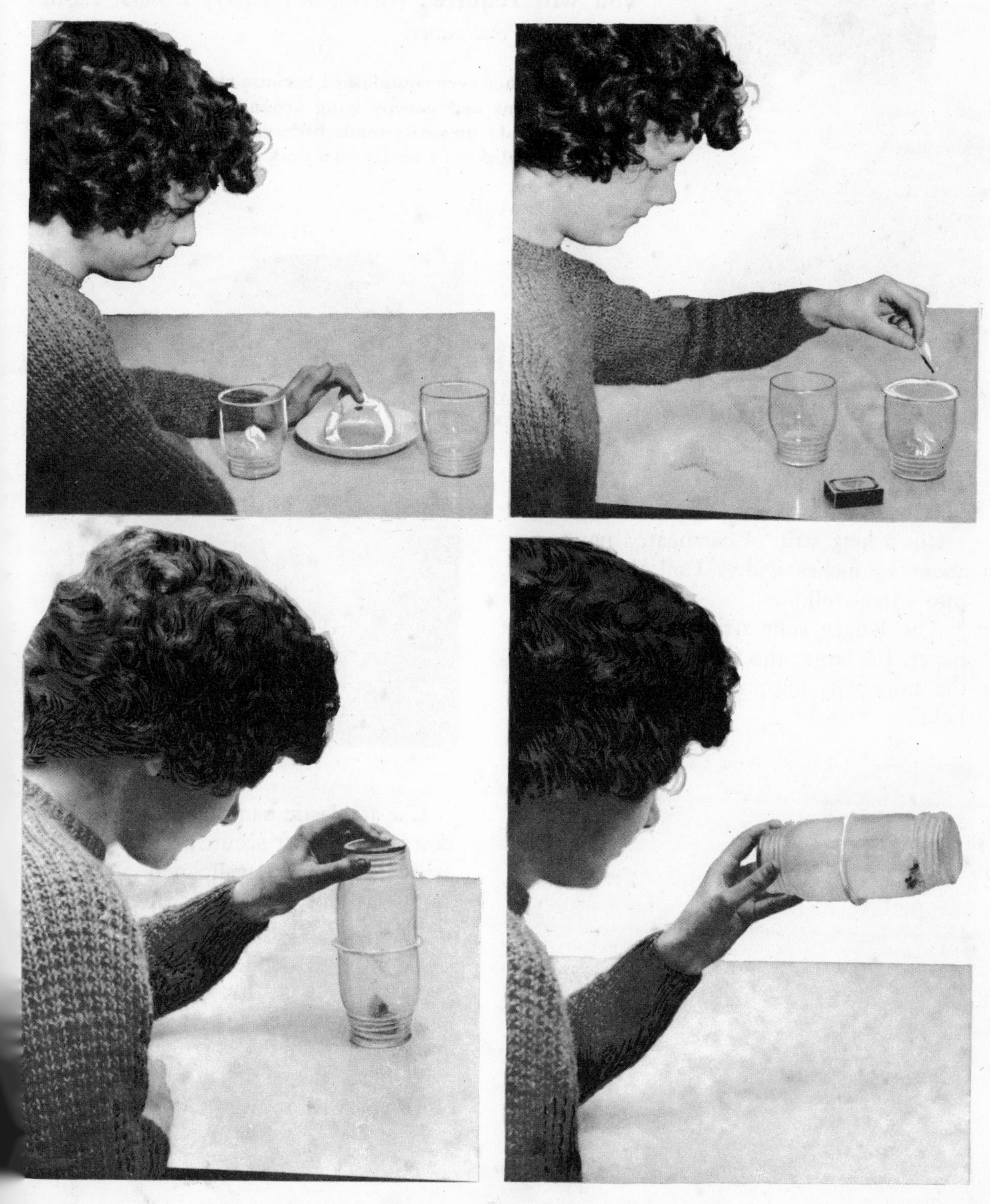

PEN AND PENCIL TIDY

You will require: *Corrugated paper, scissors, elastic band, paste, wallpaper.*

HAS Mother ever complained because she is always finding your pens and pencils lying around? Then this is just what you need: an easily made little gadget that will hold all your pens and pencils neatly on a desk or shelf.

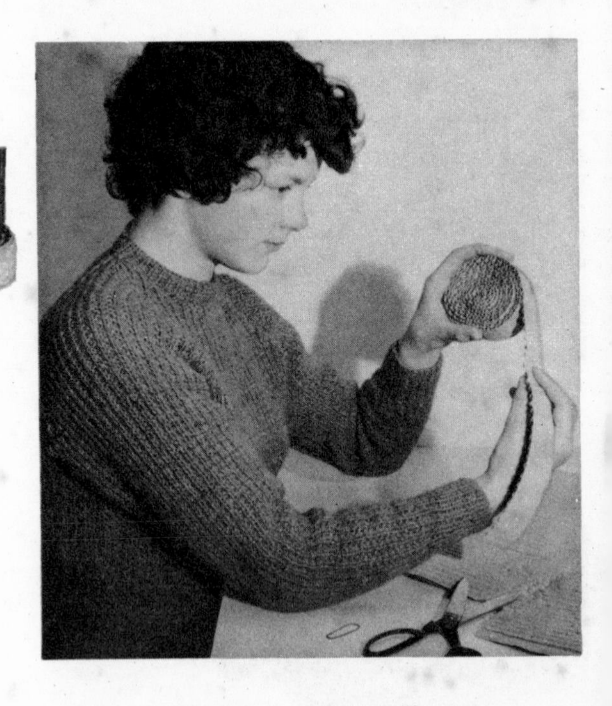

Cut a long strip of corrugated paper, about $1\frac{1}{2}$ inches wide. Coil this strip into a tight roll.

The longer your strip of corrugated paper, the larger the resulting roll—and the more pens and pencils your tidy will hold.

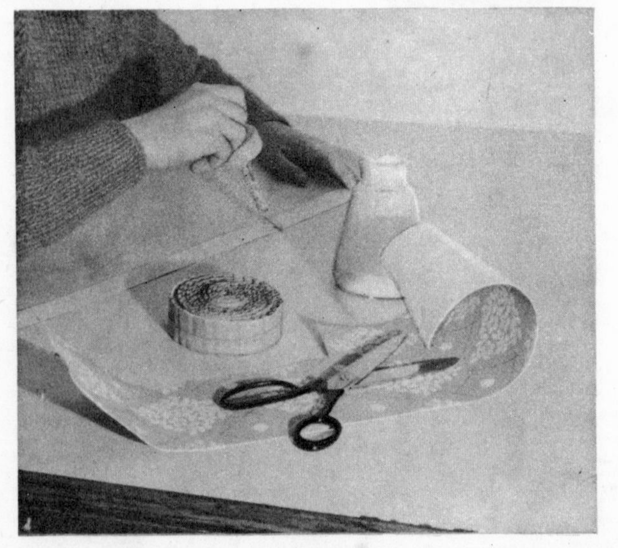

Use an elastic band to hold the coil of corrugated paper secure while you cut a strip of coloured wallpaper, and paste this so that it will serve to decorate the outside of your tidy.

When the strip of wallpaper has been secured to the outside of the coil, simply push your pencils, point downwards, into the top of the corrugated coil. It will hold them there, quite securely, until you wish to use them.

MAKING BUBBLES

You will require: *A short length of wire, glycerine, soap-flakes.*

MOST of us at some time or another have tried our hand at blowing bubbles. Unfortunately, those cheap clay pipes which used to be so admirable for our bubble-blowing are fast disappearing from the shops. There would seem to be but little demand for them from smokers these days.

However, it is still possible to spend an interesting half an hour or so making bubbles, especially if you add a teaspoonful of glycerine to a strong mixture of water and soap-flakes. Use a fork or an egg-whisk to beat the glycerine, soap-flakes and water together. It will make a mixture from which you can produce strong, beautifully coloured bubbles.

But how to make your bubbles without a pipe? Simple enough. Take a piece of wire about six to eight inches long. Form a loop on one end about the size of a penny. Bend the other end over to make a comfortable handle. (Fig. 1.)

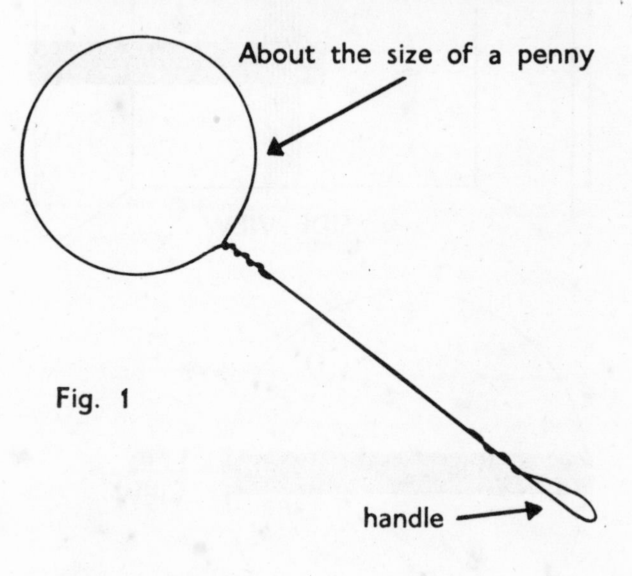

Fig. 1

Now dip the loop of wire into your glycerine and soap solution. As you withdraw it you will notice a thin film of the solution suspended in the loop. Gently wave the wire backwards and forwards, and a stream of bubbles will issue from the loop. You will find it an easy matter to catch some of the bubbles in the wire loop as they float downwards again.

COTTON-REEL CANNONS

You will require : *Cotton reels, elastic bands, thread, match-boxes, pencil, match-sticks.*

IF you should ever feel like playing an exciting shooting game one day, try making a few cotton-reel cannons.

Obtain some empty cotton reels and elastic bands. Cut the bands in one place, so that they become single strips of elastic. Secure one end of this strip of elastic to each side of a cotton reel by binding it tightly with thread. The middle of the elastic should fall across one end of the narrow hole running through the centre of the reel, as shown in Fig. 1.

Having made your cannons, the next step is to produce some targets at which to shoot. Empty match-boxes make excellent targets. With a black crayon or pencil award a number to each box.

Now stand your targets up at one end of a table. Each player is allowed two shots in succession. He scores the number of each box that he succeeds in knocking over with a well-aimed match-stick fired from his cotton-reel cannon. You will no doubt find it an easy matter to knock targets over at the beginning of the game, but it becomes progressively more difficult as fewer targets remain standing. The player knocking over the last target should be allowed a bonus of double the score shown on the side of the target.

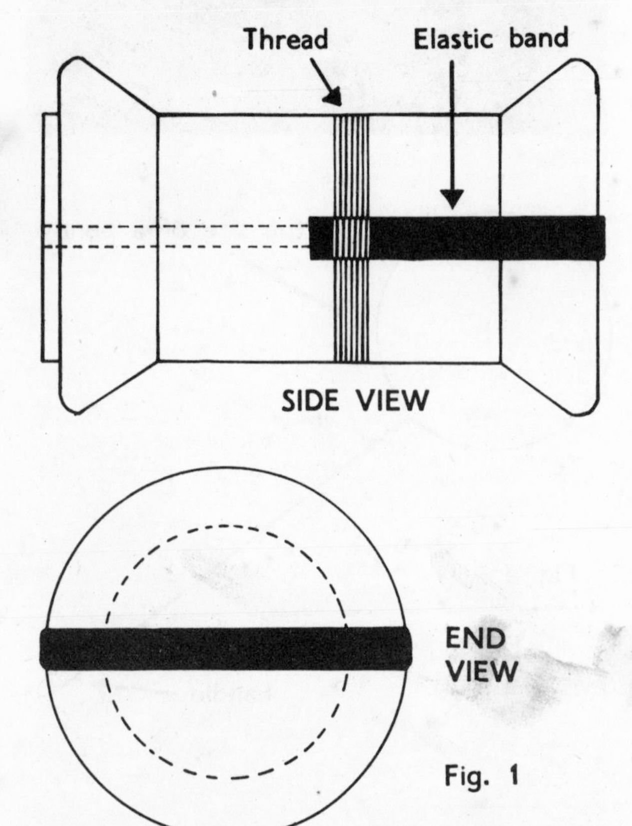

Fig. 1

THE MAGNETIC BALLOONS

You will require : *Two or three balloons.*

HAVE you ever heard of static electricity? We can charge a balloon with static electricity. It is done by the simple process of rubbing the balloon firmly against some cloth. This friction produces the electricity. In Fig. 1 you can see Robert rubbing the balloon against the back of Pauline's jumper.

After rubbing the balloon in this manner for about a minute you will find that it will attract many small objects such as hairs, feathers, etc.

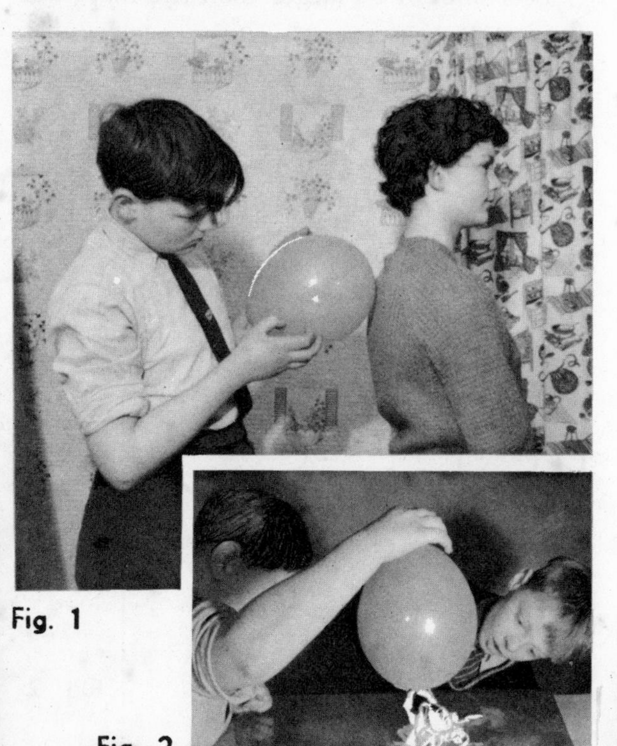

Fig. 1

Fig. 2

Figure 2 shows Robert demonstrating the powers of his magnetic balloon to Stephen. First, Robert tore some thin pieces of tissue-paper into long strands and made a loose heap of them on the table. Having charged his balloon with electricity, he then held it above the tissue-paper. As you can see, the strands leapt upwards until they touched the balloon, and were then held in that position for several seconds.

Another use for magnetised balloons is when decorating a room for a party, or at Christmas. Normally, balloons blown up by the mouth are heavier than air and fall to the ground. A balloon which has been magnetised in the manner previously described, however, will remain in position on the ceiling for quite some time, if left undisturbed.

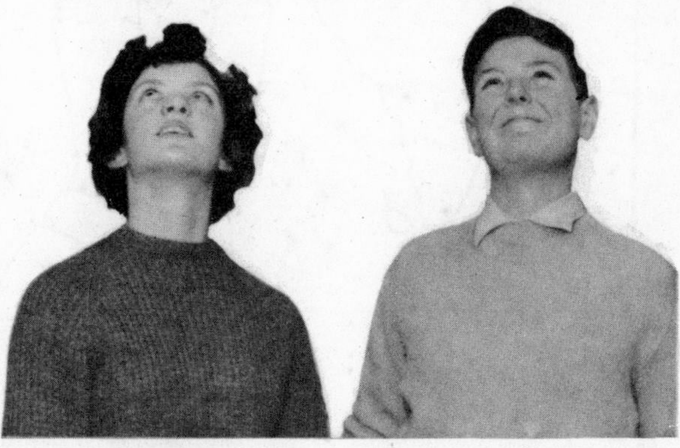

RELIEF MAP

You will require: *Plywood, fretsaw, hammer, nails, plaster of Paris, pencil, brush and paints, paste.*

I KNOW that many of you are likely to have some especial interest in countries other than the British Isles. You may have friends or relatives working or living abroad. Or, perhaps, you have always had a secret longing to visit some particular country.

It is a good idea to make a large relief map of that country and use it as the focal point of interest on one of the walls of your room. Of course, you can produce a relief map of the British Isles if you wish—or make up your own map of some unexplored "Treasure Island" which you can *explore* as you proceed with your map-making.

Young Robert decided to make himself a map of South America. Any stories about the vast, impenetrable jungles around the River Amazon, and the many fierce, strange Indian tribes that live there, have always appealed to him.

First, he obtained a large piece of plywood, although hardboard would have proved as suitable. On this he sketched in the outline of his map, drawing the coastline as carefully and as accurately as possible. (Fig. 1.)

The next thing is to draw a suitable outline around the actual map. This second outline will be the shape of the finished base of your relief map. The base should be larger than the map, but

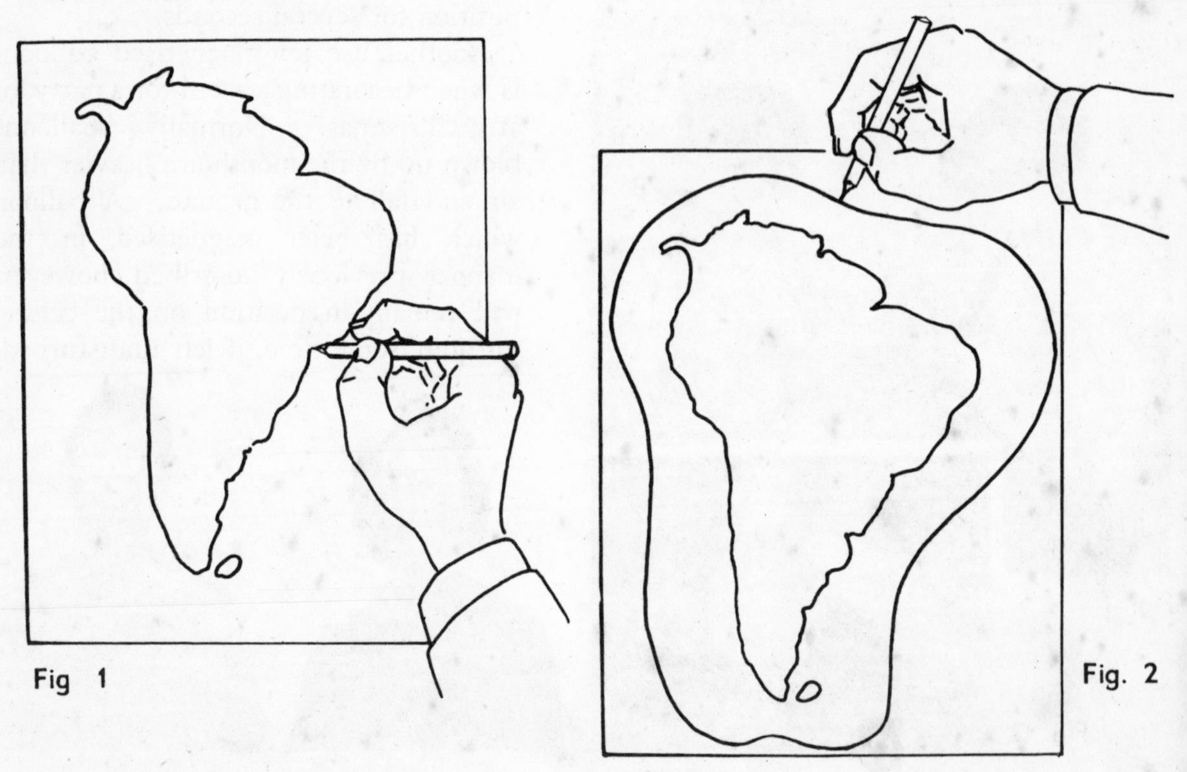

Fig 1

Fig. 2

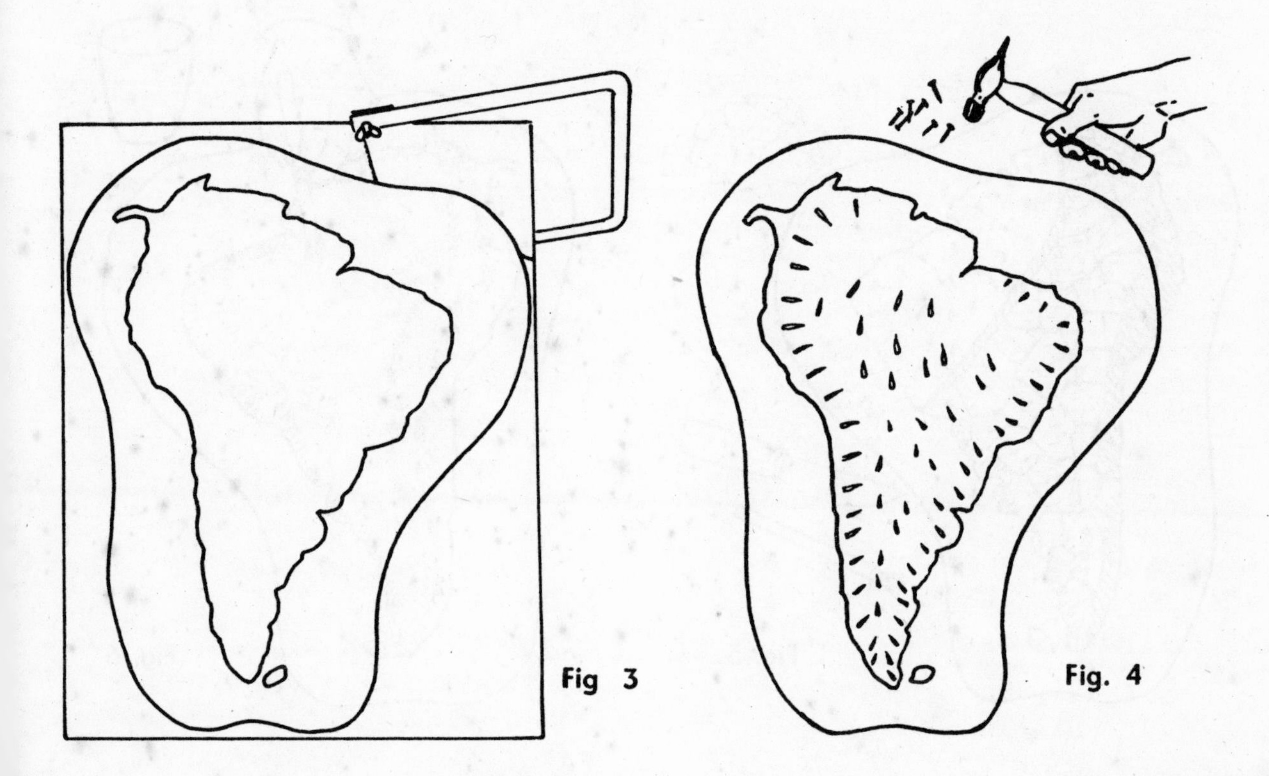

need not necessarily be square or rectangular. In fact, you will find it quite a good idea to make the shape of the base have some relation to the outline of the map. (Fig. 2.)

Use a fretsaw to remove the waste wood surrounding the base of your map. Hold the frame of the fretsaw perfectly upright when using it. Work slowly and carefully along the outline. Do not apply too much pressure to the saw, otherwise you may break the thin blade. (Fig. 3.)

Now to provide a " key " for the build-up of the land. This is easily achieved by driving nails up through the map area so that their points project and thus provide a foundation to grip the papier mâché used to raise the land above the base.

The nails should be put fairly closely around the coast-line (say every inch) and their points bent over slightly away from the sea. More nails should then be driven up at regular intervals over the remainder of the map-area. (Fig. 4.)

Next, tear one or two old newspapers into small pieces and begin pasting them

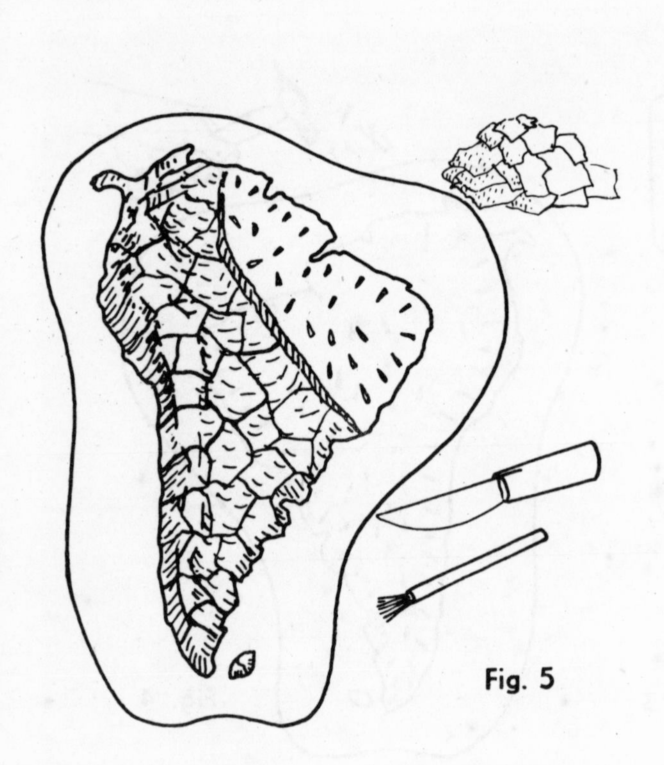
Fig. 5

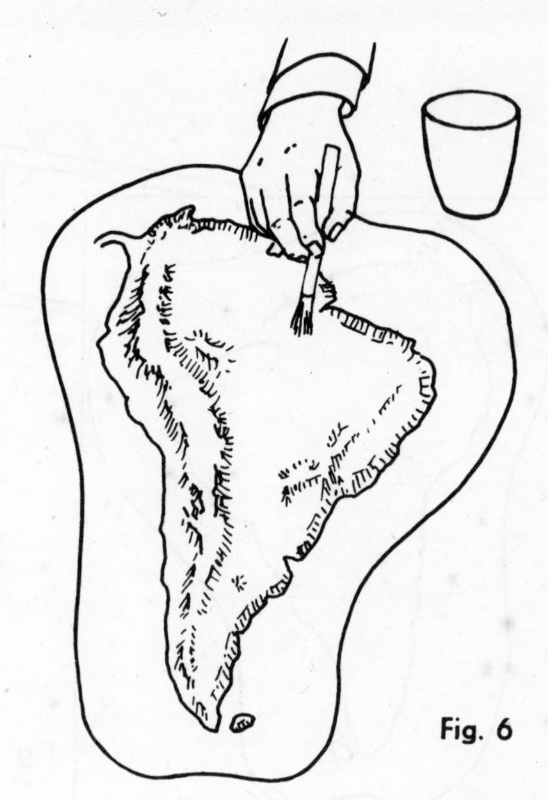
Fig. 6

all over the map, pressing them down so that they are impaled upon the points of the nails. You will need to look at your atlas frequently so that you will know just where to apply thicker layers of pasted paper in order to build up the mountainous regions.

Do not apply too much paste to the pieces of newspaper. Have just sufficient to make the various layers stick firmly to each other. An old knife is useful to press the papier mâché securely to the base without any danger of hurting your fingers on the nail-points. (Fig. 5.)

Allow time for the completed layers of paper to dry out. This may require a full twenty-four hours in a warm room. Mix a small quantity of plaster of Paris into a creamy paste and brush all over the surface of the land area. If you find that some of the mountains on your map could be improved by making them higher, this can be done by brushing more plaster in the required positions.

You will find that the plaster provides a harder and far more lifelike surface to your map than the layers of paper. (Fig. 6.)

Ordinary water-colours can be used to paint your relief map. Paint the sea area a bright green-blue, with white around the coast, and the land in green and browns. Allow the first coat of water-colour to dry and then apply a second coat. This will ensure nice strong colours.

Details of towns and cities, rivers, lakes and land boundaries, must now be marked in. This can be done with a fine brush dipped in black paint, but an easier way is to use a ball-point pen. When all details have been marked, give the complete map—sea and land areas—two coats of clear varnish. And there you will have a glossy relief map that will attract all your friends' attention when they see it.

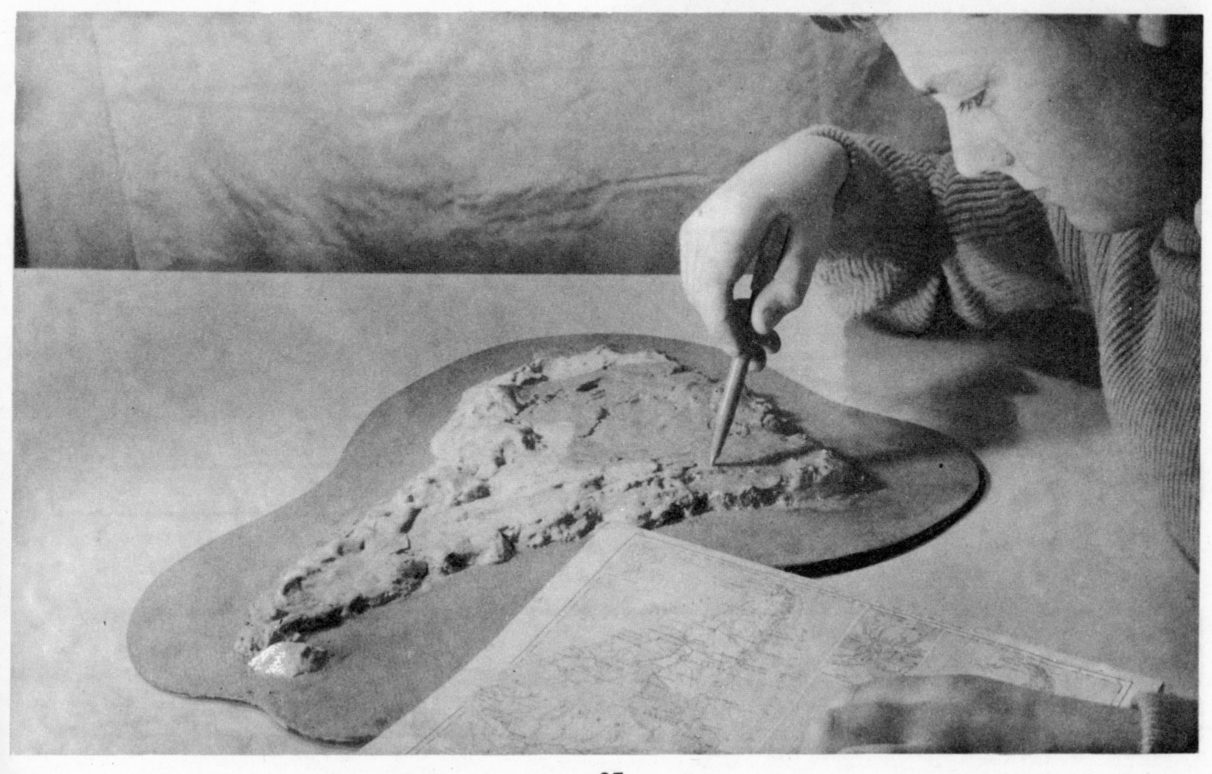

WALLPAPER BEADS

You will require: *Scraps of wall-paper, paste, scissors, knitting-needle, thin twine.*

MOST households have a few scraps of wallpaper left over from past decorating jobs. It is possible to make attractive beads, with the aid of wall-paper and paste.

Obtain as many different remnants of brightly coloured wallpaper, as possible. Cut these into long strips, about 10 to 12 inches long by ½ inch to 1 inch wide

It is possible to vary the shape of the finished bead by altering the shape of the wallpaper strip. The diagram at Fig. 1 shows several alternatives. Try one or two and see which give you the most pleasing results.

Fig. 1

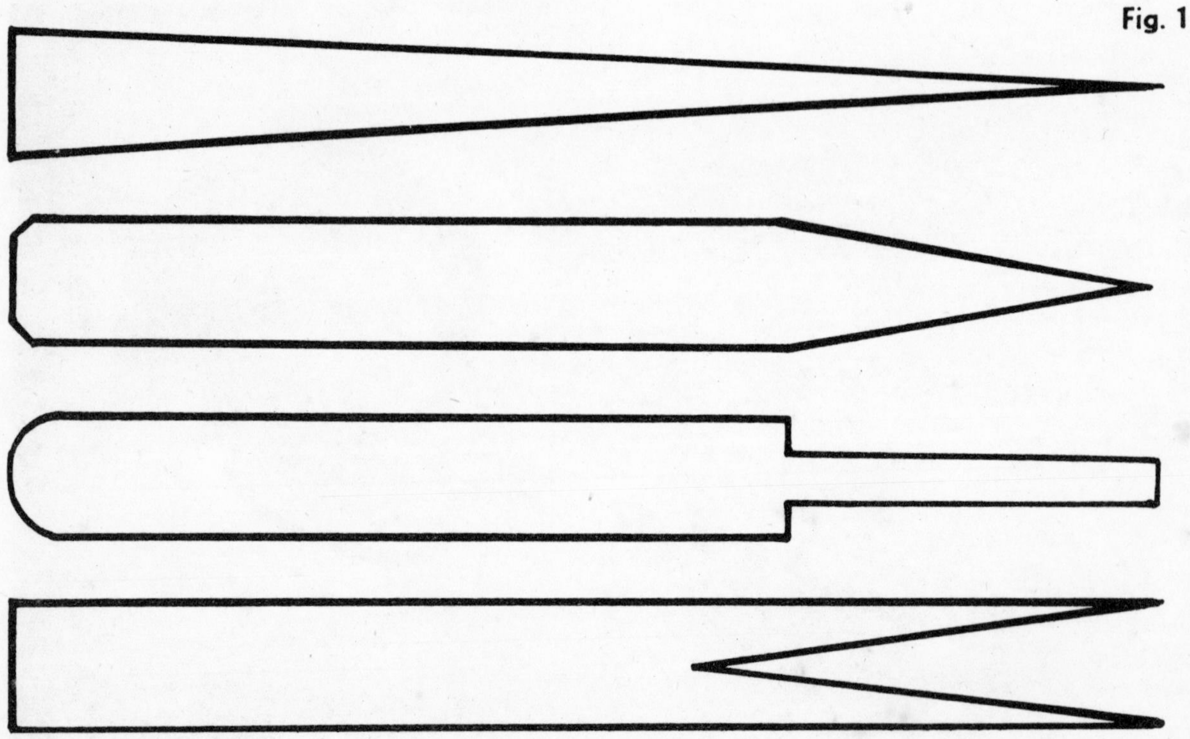

Place the strips of wallpaper face down on a sheet of scrap paper. Paste them carefully.

The beads are formed by winding the pasted strip of paper around a thin knitting-needle. You will soon see how the size and shape of the beads are affected by differences in the length and width of the wallpaper strip. Make sure that the strip is wound tightly and that the end is pasted securely down.

Fill two or three knitting-needles with beads. Allow time for the paste to dry and then carefully slide them off the needles. Finish the beads with a coat of clear varnish.

All that remains is to thread your beads upon a suitable length of thin twine or strong thread. Larger beads can be used to form a pendant, if desired. When you have made several necklaces, try making bracelets, brooches, belts, etc., from these gay, wallpaper beads.

PLASTER PLATE PLAQUES

You will require: *An old picture book, scissors, water, jam-jar, plaster of Paris, fountain pen, file, plate or saucer, paper clip.*

THESE plaques are so simple to make that even the very youngest of our readers will have no difficulty with them. On the other hand, they are so fascinating to make, and so decorative, that you must not be surprised if Mother and Father decide to try their hand.

The main material required is plaster of Paris. This can be bought quite cheaply at most builders' merchants. An ordinary plate or saucer is used as a mould from which to cast your plaque.

First, you must choose a suitable illustration for the front of your plaque. Cut the picture to size so that it neatly fits into the bottom of the saucer or plate to be used as a mould.

Dip the picture into a bowl of water. Shake or wipe off any surplus moisture. Place the picture face down in the centre of the mould. Use a pen to mark the edge of the plate to show where the top of the plaque will be.

Half fill a jam-jar with water. Add plaster of Paris, stirring gently until the mixture has reached a creamy consistency. Pour the plaster on top of the picture, taking care to ensure that no plaster flows *between* the picture and the plate. Fill the plate with plaster to within half an inch of the edge.

Tap the mould gently all round to help release any air which has become trapped in the plaster. After two or three minutes, when the plaster has set a little firmer, press a paper-clip half-way beneath the surface, making sure that it is in the correct position on your plaque—

as indicated by the ink mark previously made on the edge of the plate.

Allow the plaster some 30 minutes or so in which to set perfectly hard. Then, with the aid of a thin-bladed knife, lift the plaque free from the plate, taking care not to chip the edge of the freshly set plaster.

Should you be unlucky enough to break the edge of your plaque when freeing it from the mould, you will find it a simple enough matter to file the edge perfectly smooth again.

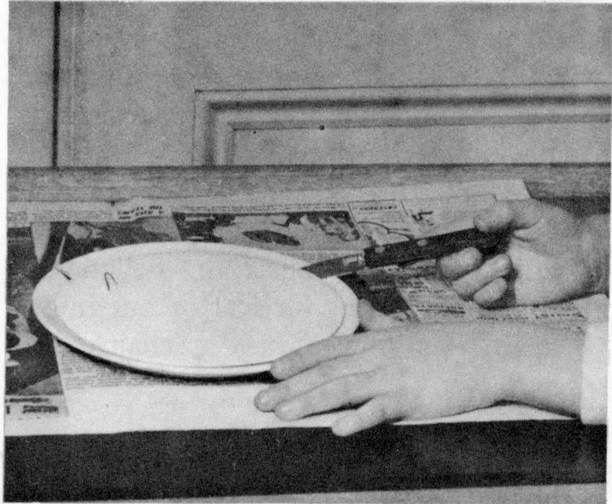

These plaster plate plaques would make nice gifts for your friends and relatives. At Christmas time, the addition of a small calendar pad would make them most welcome.

That part of the front of the plaque surrounding the picture can either be left in its natural smooth, white state or it can be painted with a gay little border. A final coat of clear varnish right over the plaster, and the picture presents quite a professional finish.

Below: Inset picture shows the completed plaque.

BALLOON AUNT SALLIES

You will require: *Balloons, brush, paints, soap.*

HOW many times have you been to a fun-fair and paid out a great deal of hard-earned pocket-money for the pleasure of throwing some balls at Aunt Sally shies? Well, here is the chance to make your own Aunt Sally for very little cost indeed.

The Aunt Sallies are really ordinary balloons on which you paint some really funny faces. You can do this with the colours from your paint-box, providing you rub your brush over a piece of soap before dipping it into the colour. You will find that the soap will help your water-colours to "take" on the rubber surface of the balloons.

First, you must inflate the balloons. Do not overdo this for fear of bursting them all before you have a chance of giving each a funny face. Tie the mouth-pieces of the balloons securely, and then prepare your paints—not forgetting that piece of soap!

The diagrams at Fig. 1 will give you some idea of the funny faces that can be painted on your balloons.

When you are quite satisfied with the faces, rub a damp brush on a piece of soap and then dip it into the colour. Transfer this direct to the surface of the balloons, painting with bold strokes of the brush.

When all the balloons have been painted, take them out into the garden and tie them at regular intervals to a broom-handle or a long cane. Support the cane on the backs of two chairs or cross two shorter canes to form supports at each end, as shown in Fig. 2.

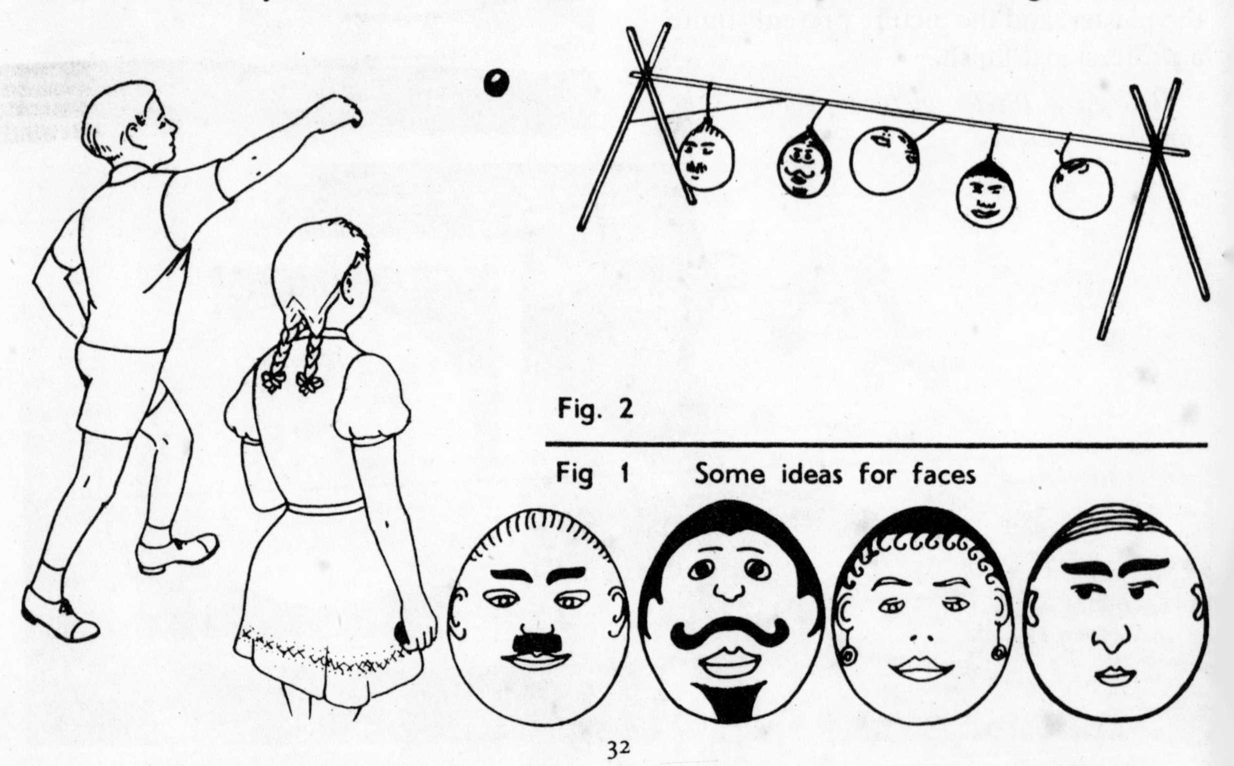

TABLE-TENNIS BAT

You will require: *Plywood, nails, fretsaw, glasspaper, file, hammer, glue.*

IT is a simple matter to make your own table-tennis bat—moreover, one that is light and easy to use.

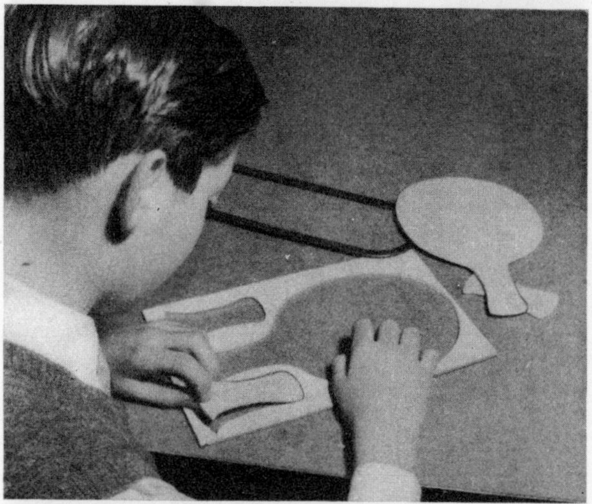

Copy the simple outlines shown in Fig. 1, drawing them on the surface of a suitably sized piece of plywood (minimum size 11 inches by 8 inches). Perhaps you can use a small plate or a compass to help you draw the circular part of the bat. The grid of inch squares will show you the actual size and shape required.

Hold the plywood firmly over the edge of a bench or table and use a fretsaw to cut out the bat and the two handle-pieces.

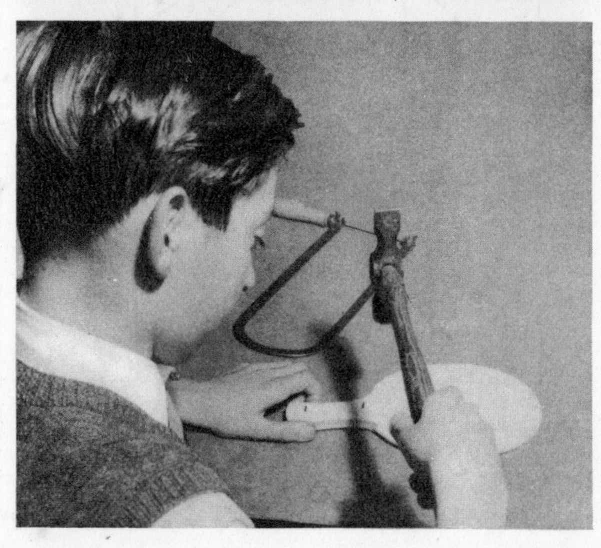

Remove the various pieces as you cut them out. Care should be taken to saw exactly along the lines you have drawn. This will save you time when it comes to filing the edges of your bat perfectly smooth. Photo shows the second handle-piece being removed from the waste wood.

Fig. 1 Each square represents one inch.

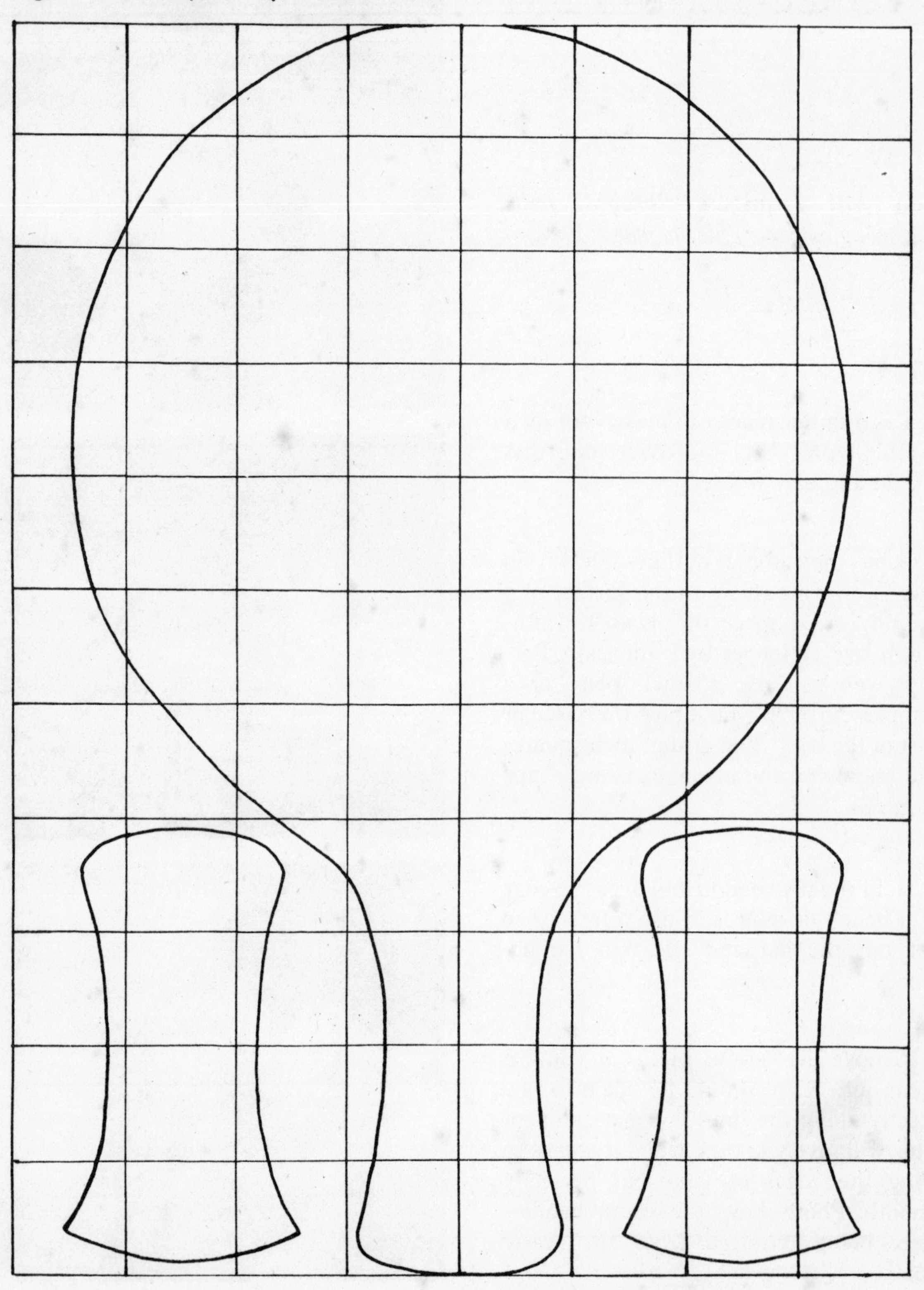

Now position the handle-pieces on the bat and secure them with small nails. Use short nails that are not likely to go right through the handle and stick out the other side. Short nails can be driven in from each side of the handle, securing the two pieces firmly to the bat.

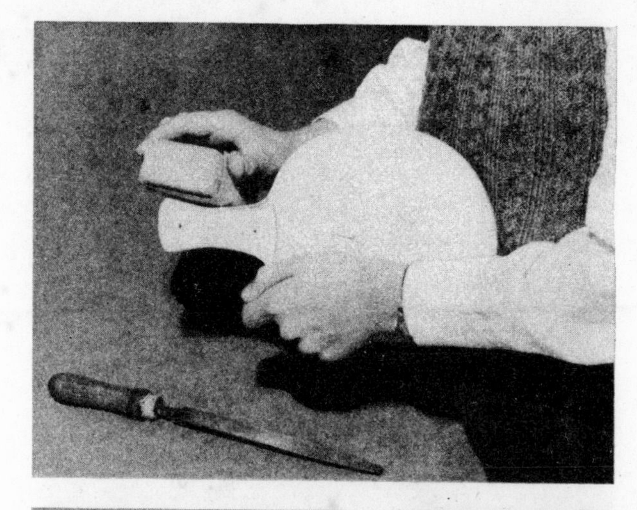

Use a file and glasspaper to clean up the edges of the table-tennis bat. Particular care should be taken to ensure that the handle is perfectly smooth. Round off the sawn edges of the handle so that it fits comfortably in the hand.

The blade of your bat must now receive a covering of fine glasspaper on each side. This enables the bat to grip the ball in play, giving it " spin." Use No. 1 or No. 0 glasspaper. Draw round the edge of the bat, with the outline appearing on the back of a sheet of glass-paper placed beneath the bat.

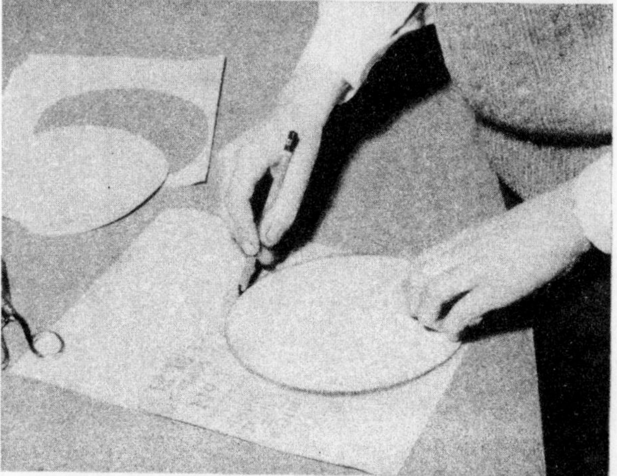

These glasspaper coverings must be the same size as the bat and should fit snugly above the handle.

Place the glasspaper, face down on a sheet of newspaper, spread balsa cement or gum evenly over the reverse side. Position the glasspaper cut-outs, one on each side of the bat. Use sharp scissors to trim off any overhanging parts. Place the completed bat under a pile of heavy books until the cement or gum has set.

Apply a coat of clear varnish to the handle and the edge of the blade and your bat is ready for use.

THE IMPOSSIBLE POUND NOTE

You will require : *A one-pound note.*

❧ ❧ ❧

YOUNG Robert had received such tremendous wealth on his birthday that he was more than a little inclined to show off. Pauline told him that she would probably be able to do far more good with a pound note than he could.

Robert promptly offered her the pound providing she could pick it up from the floor without moving her feet. Pauline first made quite sure that she would not be stood on one side of the room with the pound note on the floor on the other side. Then she agreed to have a try.

Robert asked her to stand against the wall, with her heels actually touching the wall. He then placed the pound note on the floor about 12 inches in front of her.

To Pauline's surprise, she was unable to pick that note up without moving her feet. Our illustration shows her trying a cunning little sideways movement—but without success.

P.S. This is not a rich man's trick. Try it with a penny instead of a pound note.

GIVING PAPER MUSCLES

You will require: *Three tumblers, drawing-paper.*

"HERE are three tumblers and a square of drawing-paper," Robert told Pauline. "All you have to do is support one of the tumblers between the other two, using the sheet of paper to hold the first tumbler aloft."

"Do I tell Mother it's your fault or mine, when the tumbler falls and breaks?" asked Pauline.

"The tumbler won't fall," Robert assured her. "Watch this."

He then folded the paper in zigzag concertina fashion, as shown at Fig. 1. This is what puts "muscles" into the paper, making it so strong that it can support quite heavy weights.

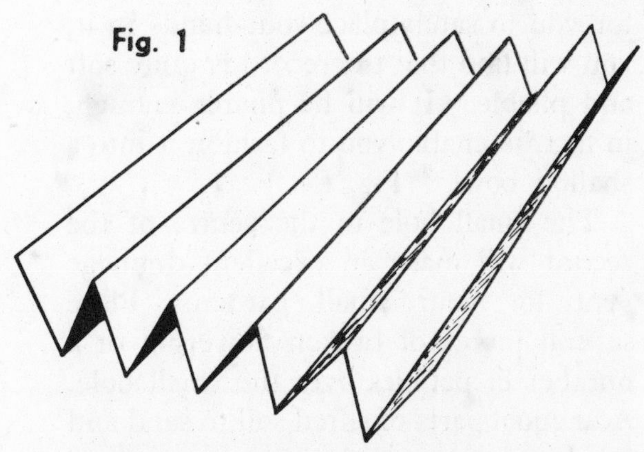
Fig. 1

With his folding completed, Robert placed the ends of the paper on the two tumblers so that it formed a miniature bridge between them. He then carefully placed the third tumbler on top of the paper. As you can see the folded paper easily supported the tumbler.

TABLE GARDENS

You will require: *Old gramophone record or small bowl, soil, sand, pebbles, modelling-clay, pieces of glass or mirror, cacti and small plants.*

MANY people living in flats or similar accommodation have no gardens of their own. One of these charming little table gardens would make a wonderful present for such folks. The gardens would also be greatly appreciated by the aged and invalid, as well, of course, by everyone else who likes to see fresh, growing plants around them.

ANY small bowl or container is suitable for one of these miniature gardens. Possibly one of the simplest and most inexpensive containers can be made from an ordinary gramophone record.

Choose a large record that has outlived its usefulness. Soak it for several minutes in a bowl of really hot water. When the water has cooled sufficiently for you to safely place your hands in it, you will find that the record is quite soft and pliable. It will be pliable enough, in fact, to enable you to fashion it into a shallow bowl. (Fig. 1.)

The small hole in the centre of the record will make an excellent drainage vent for your small garden. Place several pieces of broken flowerpot or a number of pebbles over the small hole. Add equal parts of sifted soil to sand and fill the container with this mixture.

Now comes the really interesting work of arranging plants and accessories to their best effect in your small garden. Cacti and suitable dwarf plants and trees may be bought from most florists or nurserymen. If you have not too much pocket money to spare, however, you will find many attractive little plants, ferns, mosses, etc., under hedgerows or during a walk through woods or countryside.

Attractively shaped stones make wonderful imitation boulders, and small pieces of moss can be used as soft, green lawns. Fragments of glass or mirror can be made to look like really lifelike little pools and streams. (Fig. 2.)

It is possible to give each little garden its own styling. The rather bleak, but extremely natural "moorland" landscape of Fig. 2 is quite different to the bizarre little garden of Fig. 3, with its stones, coral, and model crab. You will notice, however, that both these small landscapes are housed in containers that have been fashioned from gramophone records.

Depending upon their arrangement, stones and pebbles can provide as much interest in a miniature garden as more complicated accessories modelled from clay or wax. Notice how effective a very few plants can be when arranged as a background. (Fig. 3.)

Cacti make excellent table gardens by themselves. They do not need anything elaborate for a container. The small cacti garden shown in Fig. 4 is housed in a baby's plastic building-brick. Most cacti are naturally used to cramped, arid conditions. They make excellent indoor plants because of this.

With a larger container it is possible to introduce all sorts of figures and models made from clay or modelling-wax. Small figures of men and animals,

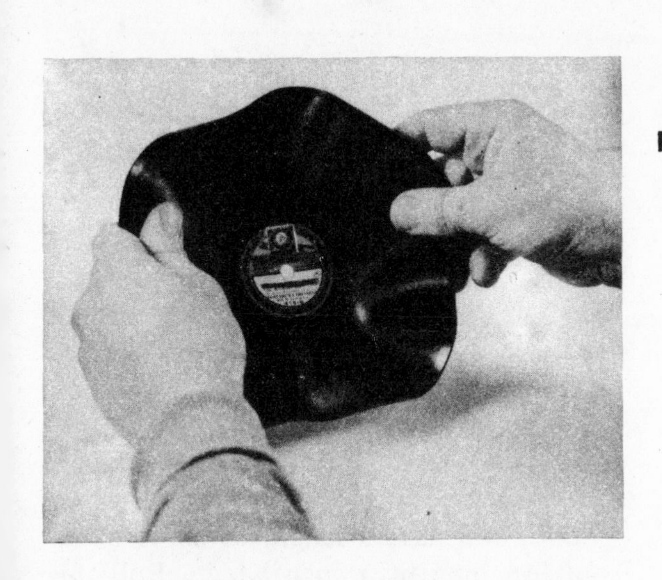

Fig. 1

Fig. 2

Fig 3

Fig. 4

Fig. 5

models of temples, bridges, and fences; little houses, wishing-wells, even miniature castles, can all be given a suitable setting in a small table garden.

Although you will find plenty of scope for originality when designing and stocking these small landscapes, care should be taken not to introduce too many models or similar accessories. Figure 5 shows a well-balanced effect achieved by careful use of plants, pebbles, and wax models.

PAPER PENCIL-HOLDER

You will require : *Coloured magazine cover, scissors, gum, stub of pencil.*

HERE is one way of using up old pencil stubs by making colourful paper holders for them.

Cut the coloured cover of an old magazine into 1-inch strips. (Fig. 1.)

Paste one strip to the end of the other until you have a length of paper about 4 feet long by 1 inch wide. Roll this long strip tightly together, and then gum the last 8 inches of the paper. (Fig. 2.)

Complete the rolling and then allow time for the gum to dry. Figure 3 shows how the roll of paper is then drawn out into the shape of a miniature telescope by pulling carefully at one end.

The stub of pencil is then pressed firmly into the wide end of the paper holder. Should the pencil stub fit rather loosely into the end of the holder it will be found quite an easy matter to gum a strip of paper around the stub to make it a tight fit.

WEEKLY 6d

Fig. 1

Fig. 2

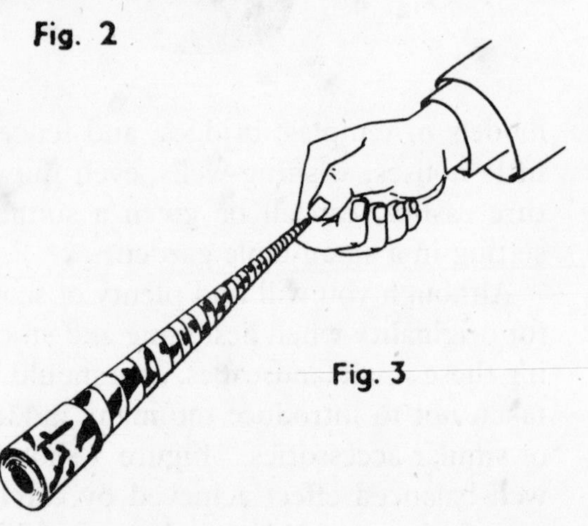

Fig. 3

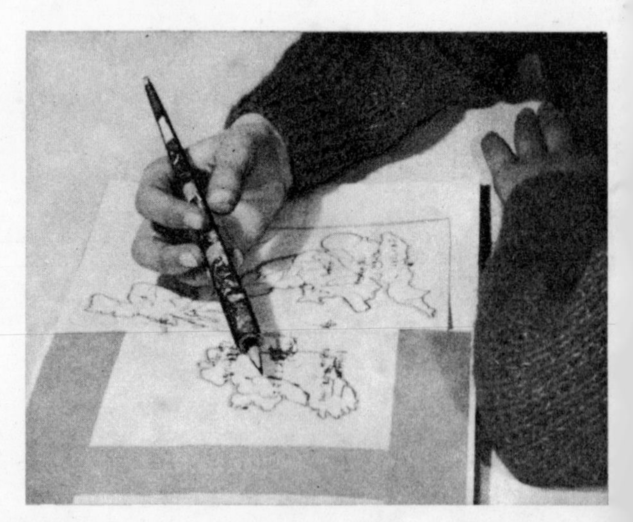

MAGIC TUMBLER

You will require : *Water, tumbler, drawing-paper.*

ROBERT and Terry have just been told something more about air pressure. They thought they would like to try a little experiment for themselves.

First, Terry filled the tumbler until it was brim full. He was thoughtful enough to place a large plate beneath the tumbler so that the table would not get wet. (Fig. 1.)

He then placed a square of strong drawing-paper on top of the tumbler, pressing it down gently to make sure that the paper touched the edge of the tumbler all the way round.

He then handed over to Robert the task of turning the tumbler upside down and raising it aloft. To their delight the air pressure on the square of paper was sufficient to hold the water in the glass (Fig. 2.) Although you cannot see it in the illustration there was a large bowl placed ready in position, in case the experiment had misfired. It is a wise precaution. Mother may not thank you for drenching her carpet—even in the cause of Science !

Fig. 1

Fig. 2

WIRE PLANT-POT HOLDER

You will require : *Wire, pliers, emery-cloth, flowerpot, enamel paint and brush.*

IT is possible to turn a length of stout wire into an attractive plant-pot holder. Handicraft shops often sell wire that is already painted or decorated in some way, but it is possible to use any length of wire salvaged from a grocer's box, etc., and effect the same transformation with it.

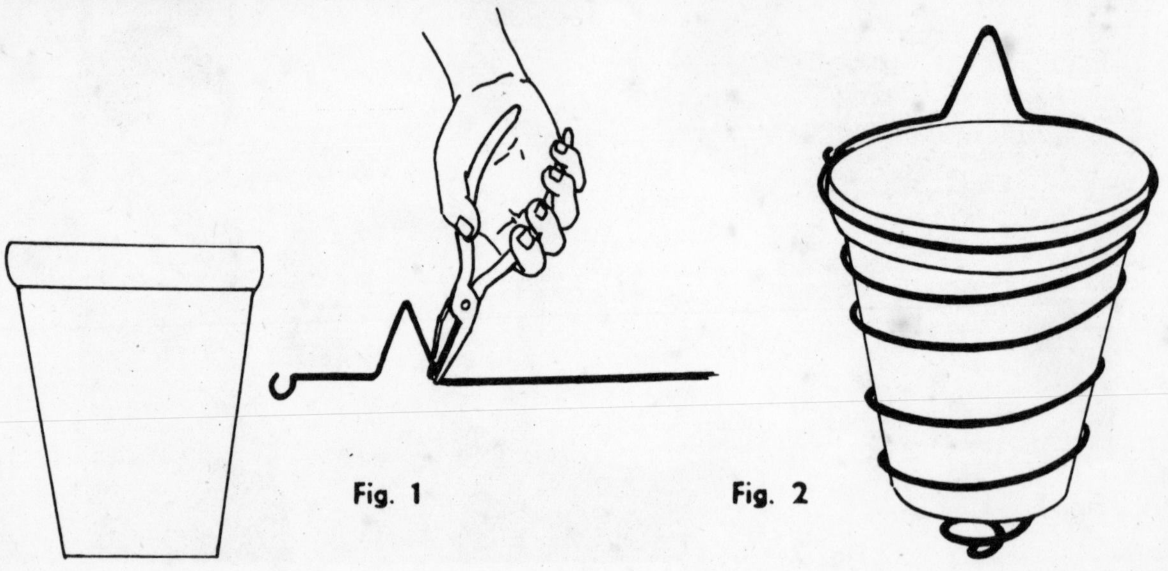

Fig. 1

Fig. 2

If the wire you have obtained for your holder is rusted or badly discoloured, place a small sheet of emery-cloth in the palm of your hand and draw the length of wire through the emery once or twice until it is clean and shining.

With the aid of a pair of pliers, bend the first 4 or 5 inches of the wire into the shape shown at Fig. 1. That means bending a small hook into the first inch of the wire, and so on, as illustrated.

Use a 5-inch diameter flowerpot to serve as a former for your wire. Bend the wire, spiral fashion, carefully around the flowerpot. (Fig. 2.)

Cut any surplus wire off, with the help of the pliers, and then bend the last part of the wire into a little ornamental coil.

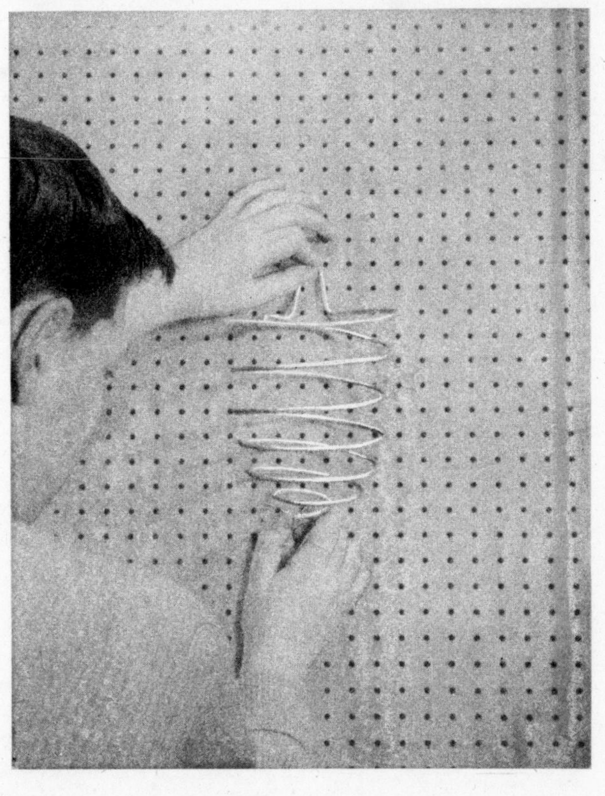

The small hook which you fashioned at the beginning of the length of wire should now be bent down so that it grips the coil below it. Picture shows how the holder should look when it is completed, with the triangular bend forming a neat hanger at the top.

Your final job before placing a plant in the wire holder will be to carefully paint the wire any colour desired. You will find these simple little plant-pot holders look most luxurious if they are given one or two coats of gold or silver paint.

WHIRLING DAZZLER

You will require : *Cardboard, compass and pencil, scissors, paints and brush, twine or thin string.*

HERE is another simple, but effective little toy for you to make. Use a compass to draw a 3 inch diameter circle on a piece of thick cardboard. If you cannot find a compass, try drawing round an upturned cup or tumbler.

Make two small holes, about $\frac{1}{2}$ inch apart, in the centre of the circle. Cut the disc out and then carefully cut a series of teeth all round the outer edge so that the disc resembles a cardboard cog-wheel.

With paints or crayons colour both sides of the disc in bright colours.

Now obtain a length of twine or thin string about a yard long. Thread one end of the string through the hole " A " and then pass the *same* end of the string back through hole " B." Tie both ends of the string together with a neat knot.

Your Whirling Dazzler is set in motion by adopting the following method. Place a finger in the loops at each end of the string. Slide the disc along until it is suspended mid-way between both hands. Now twist the disc, with a spinning motion from both wrists, until the string is tightly twisted. By pulling alternately outwards with the hands and then relaxing this pressure, you will be able to keep the disc in spinning motion with the teeth along its edge making a loud whirring sound and all the bright colours blending together to form white.

PAPER SCREECHER

You will require : *Greaseproof paper, scissors.*

MOST boys like to make a noise occasionally, and Robert is no exception.

From a piece of waxed paper, of the type used to wrap loaves of bread, he cut a piece to the same size and shape shown. By folding the paper in half, as shown by the dotted line, he was able to cut the shape quite neatly.

Holding the paper between the first two fingers of one hand, he blew strongly into the paper, which promptly gave a high-pitched screech that was not at all to Pauline's liking, as you can see.

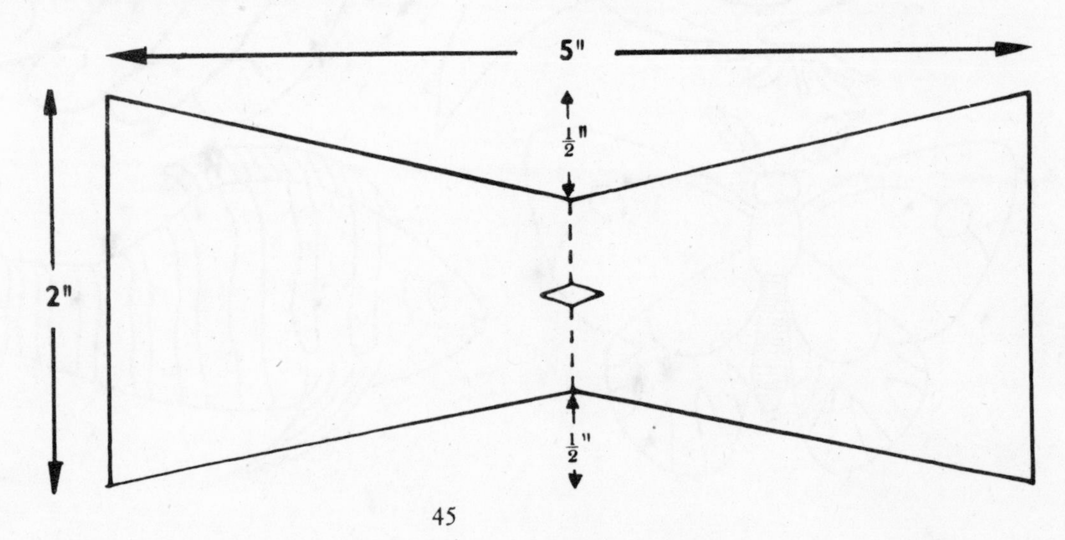

COLOURED FOIL DECORATIONS

You will require : *Cardboard, pencil, scissors, gum, coloured foil, pen and ink.*

THERE is no need to waste those beautifully coloured pieces of shiny metallic foil used to wrap your toffees and chocolates. With their aid it is possible to make some really attractive wall decorations.

You must first decide upon the type of decoration you favour. These metallic foils look particularly well when adding their shining colours to imitation fish, birds, butterflies, flowers, etc.

Begin by drawing a simple shape on a piece of thin card. Figure 1 offers a few shapes for you to copy. As you will see, we have chosen the butterfly for the remainder of our illustrations, but the others would have made as equally attractive decorations.

Once you have cut out your card shape, ink in all the main lines of the body with broad strokes of your pen. (Fig. 2.)

Now comes the interesting part of choosing your colours from the various pieces of coloured foil and silver paper

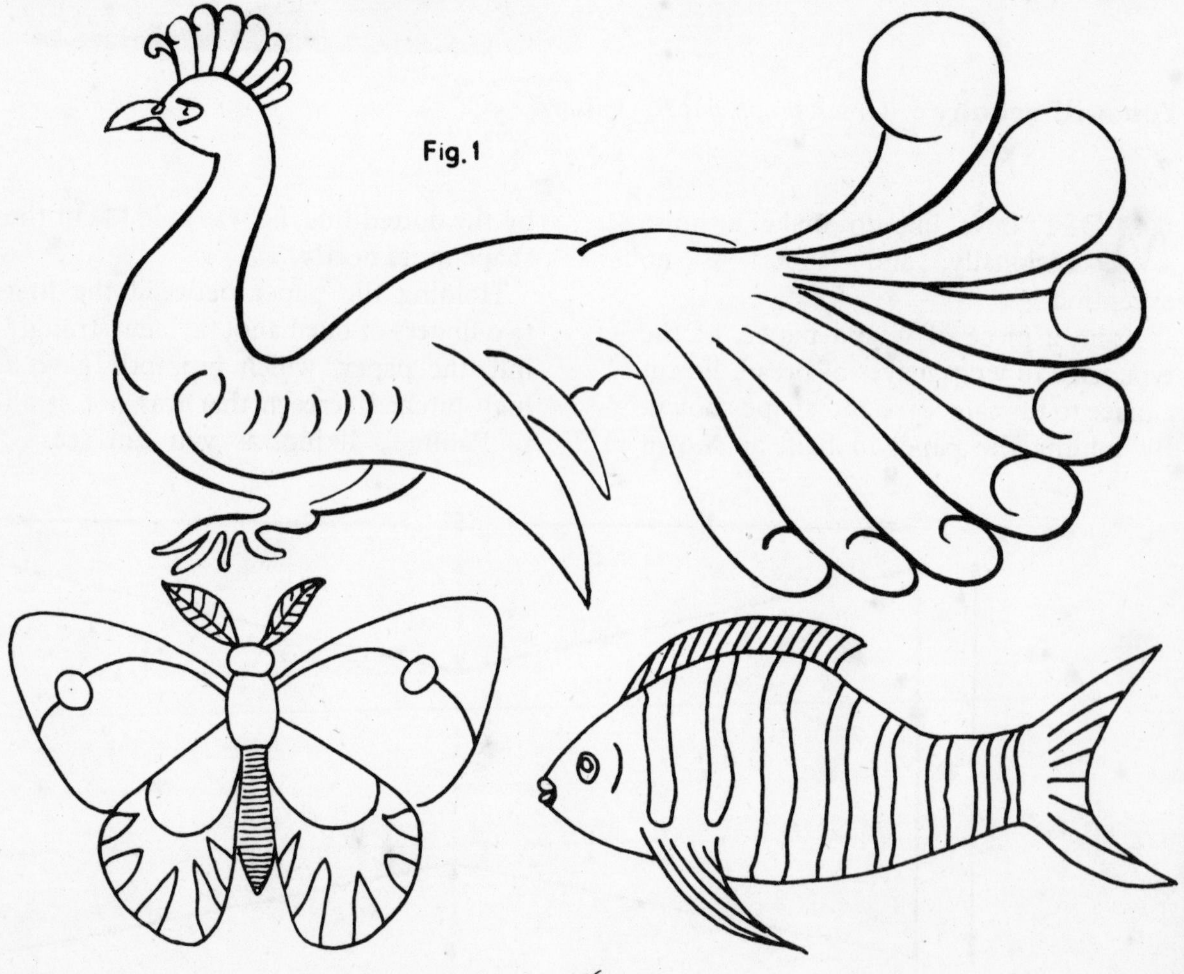
Fig. 1

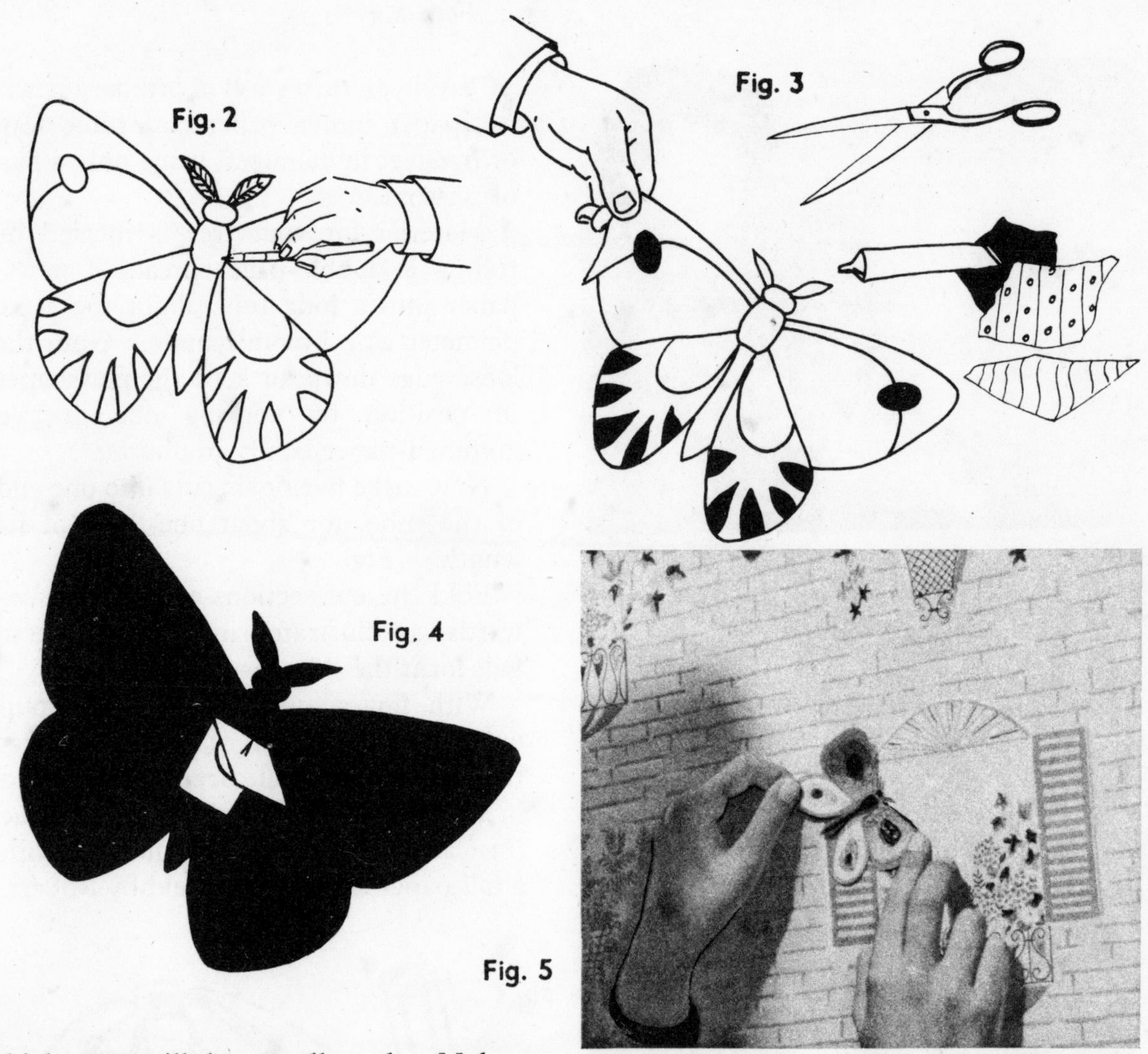

which you will have collected. Make quite sure that the papers you have chosen are large enough to cover those portions of the decoration for which you require them. Cut the different pieces of foil to the size and shape required and then glue them carefully into position on the cut-out. (Fig. 3.)

Simple hangers for your decorations can be made by folding a small piece of paper in half. Glue one half to the back of the cut-out, as shown in Fig. 4. In the free half of the paper insert a drawing-pin in such a position that it can be used to pin your completed work to the wall.

The butterfly cut-outs often look quite effective if placed somewhere close to a vase of flowers—or even made to appear as though they have just alighted on the actual blooms, themselves. The illustration at Fig. 5, however, shows how effective these decorations can look when placed on appropriate wallpaper.

A PAPER TREE

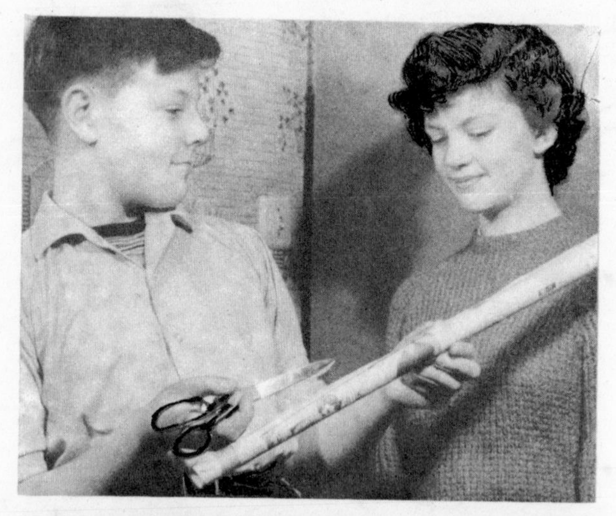

You will require : *Newspaper, gum and brush, scissors.*

CAN you turn a roll of ordinary newspaper into a paper tree some four or five feet in diameter, using only a pair of scissors ?

Material for your tree is formed by rolling a double-page spread of newspaper into a long tube about the same diameter as a broom handle. Gum the loose edge down, or keep the newspaper in position by sticking one or two gummed-paper bands around it.

Now make five or six cuts into one end of the tube, for about one-third of its length. (Fig. 1.)

Fold the cut sections of paper downwards, as illustrated in Fig. 2. These will form the " leaves " of your tree.

With finger and thumb, gently pull out the top section of leaves so that the newspaper roll begins to extend in length, telescope fashion. Continue this carefully and you will finish up with a tall paper tree like that held by Robert.

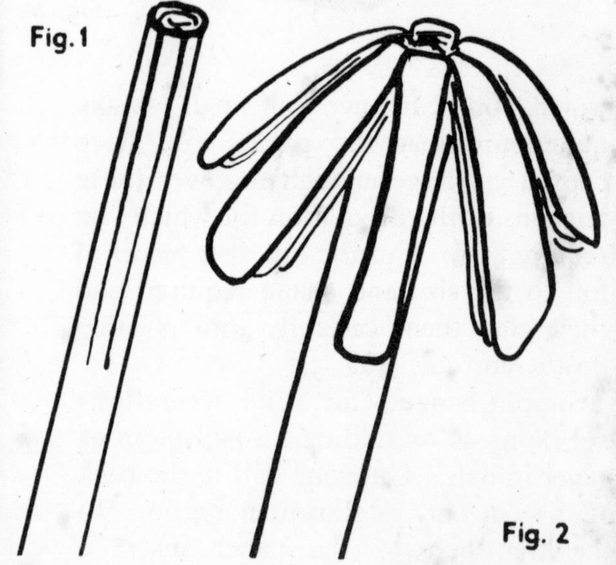

MODEL RAILWAY TUNNEL

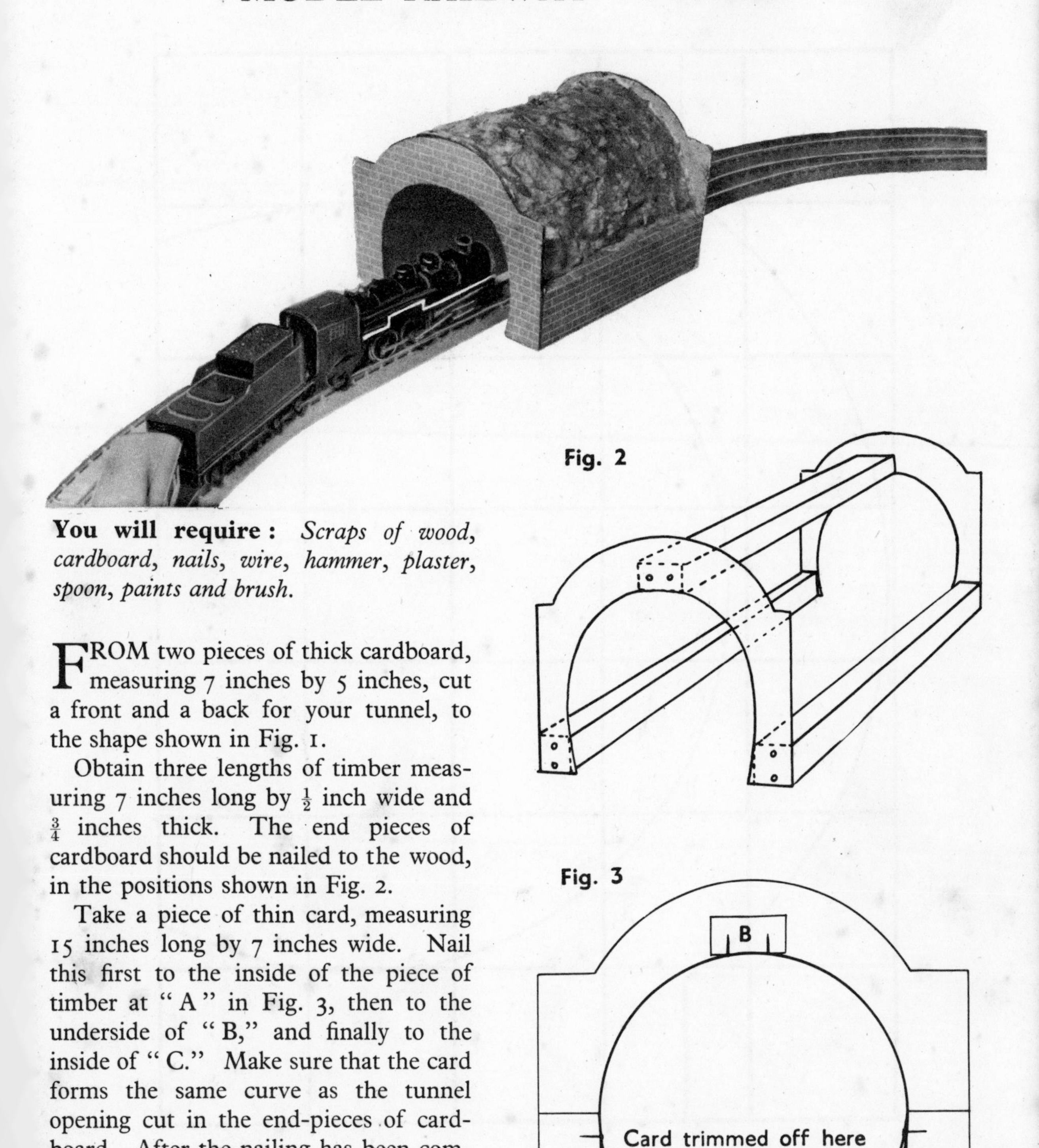

You will require: *Scraps of wood, cardboard, nails, wire, hammer, plaster, spoon, paints and brush.*

FROM two pieces of thick cardboard, measuring 7 inches by 5 inches, cut a front and a back for your tunnel, to the shape shown in Fig. 1.

Obtain three lengths of timber measuring 7 inches long by $\frac{1}{2}$ inch wide and $\frac{3}{4}$ inches thick. The end pieces of cardboard should be nailed to the wood, in the positions shown in Fig. 2.

Take a piece of thin card, measuring 15 inches long by 7 inches wide. Nail this first to the inside of the piece of timber at " A " in Fig. 3, then to the underside of " B," and finally to the inside of " C." Make sure that the card forms the same curve as the tunnel opening cut in the end-pieces of cardboard. After the nailing has been completed, any surplus card should be cut off flush with the underside of " C."

Fig. 1 Actual size.

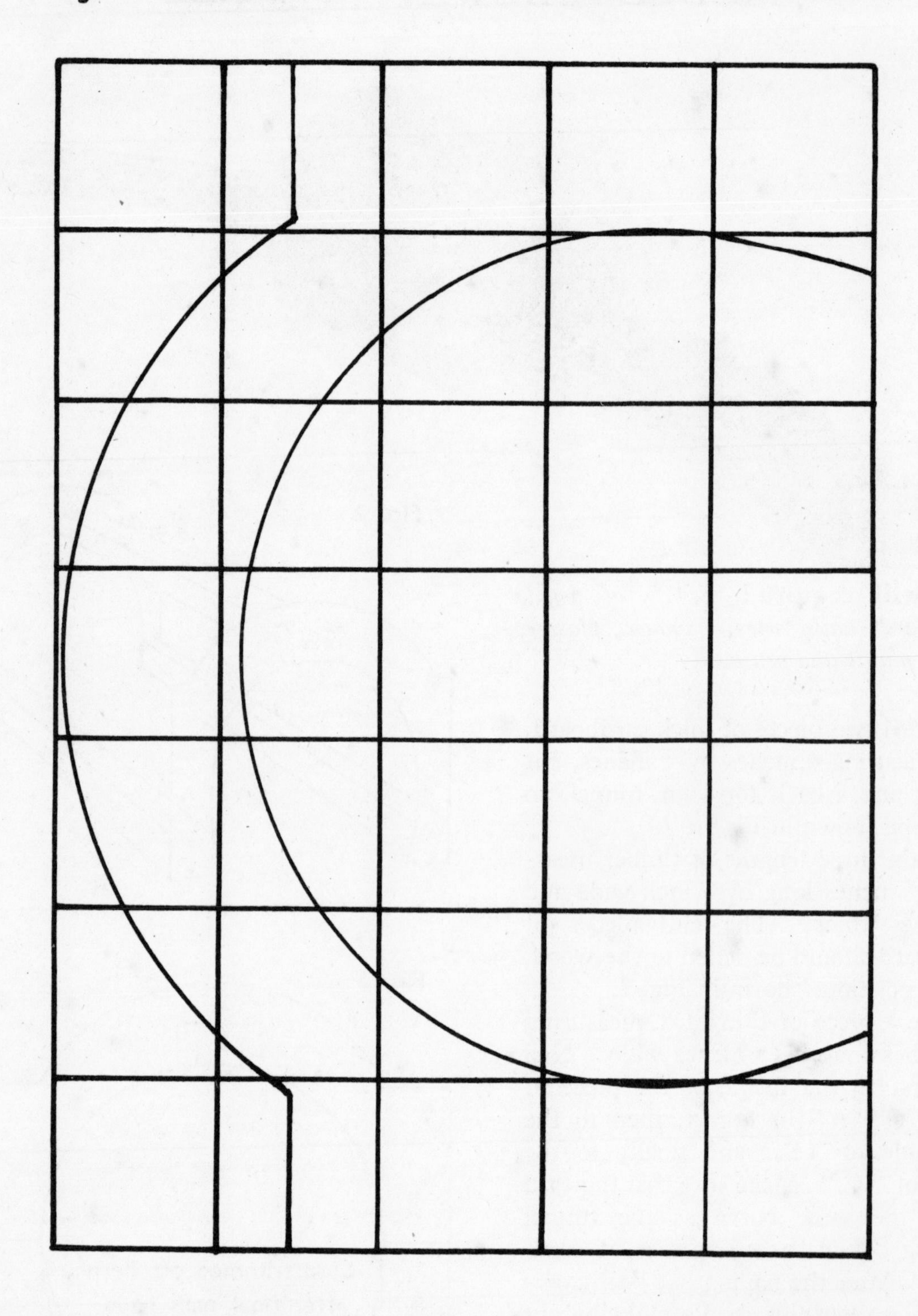

A series of small nails should now be partly driven into the upper edges of the three pieces of timber. Bind wire over the outside of the tunnel, looping it around the heads of the projecting nails, as illustrated in Fig. 4.

When the wire is extended along the full outer surface of the model tunnel, it will provide a good foundation for a plaster of Paris covering. Mix some plaster to a thick paste and spoon it over the top of the tunnel. (Fig. 5.) Do not attempt to smooth the surface but leave it quite rough. Build up this outer covering of plaster until the wire and nails are completely hidden.

Allow time for the plaster to harden, then use your paints to colour the model tunnel as realistically as possible. Deal with the inside, first. Paint this quite black—if necessary giving it two coats of paint to achieve a really dark tone.

The ends and " walls " of the tunnel can be painted to resemble brickwork (Fig. 6), whilst the plaster on the outer curved surface should be painted with greens and browns to resemble a rough grassy hillock. When satisfied with your colouring, apply one or two coats of clear varnish to preserve it.

In use, the tunnel will be found suitable for a twin-track " oo "-gauge model railway. The dimensions given here, however, can soon be altered to suit a different gauge model rolling-stock, if desired.

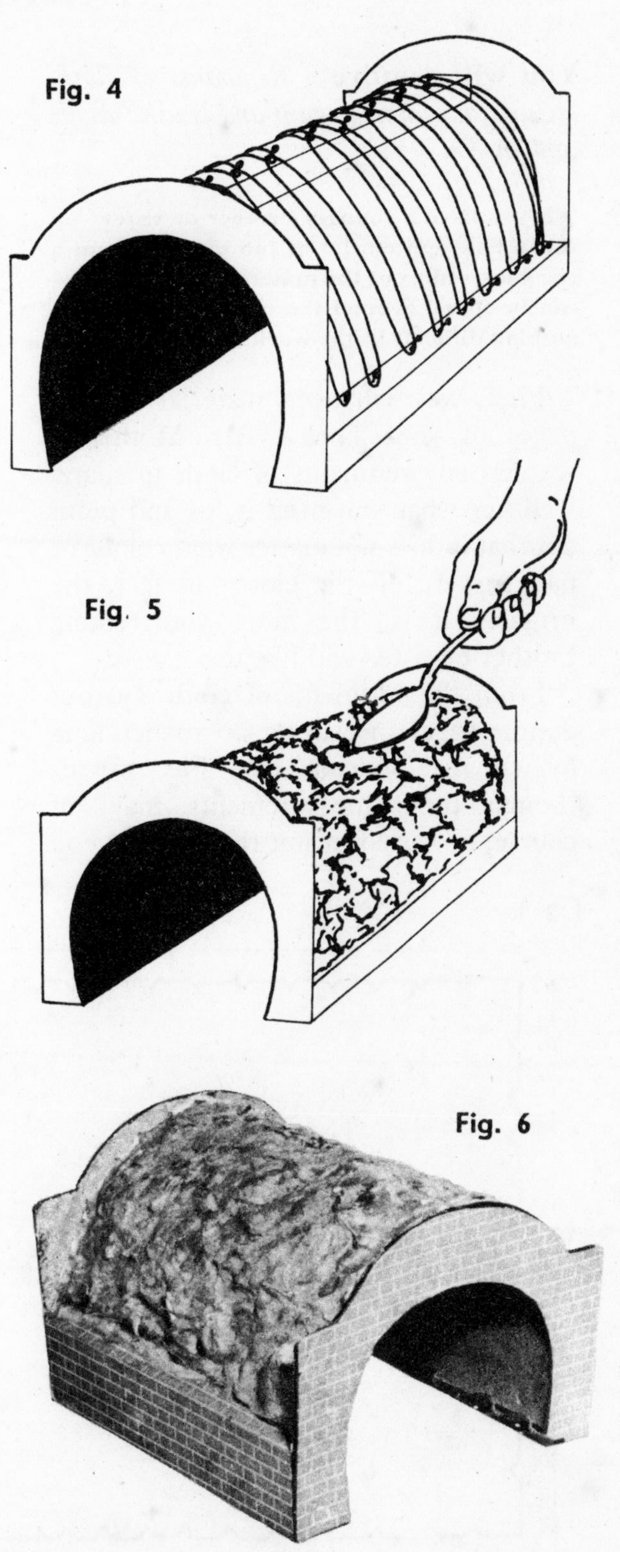
Fig. 4

Fig. 5

Fig. 6

A RAG BOOK

You will require : *Remnants of cloth, scissors, magazines, gum and brush, needle and thread.*

If you have a younger brother or sister you can have quite a lot of fun making them a rag book. Most of the materials you will need can be found around the home, and there is nothing difficult in the work involved.

First, you will need material for the pages of your book. Ask Mother if she has any remnants of cloth to spare. Tell her what you need it for and point out that it does not matter what colour or patterns are on the cloth—in fact, the brighter it is, the more your young brother or sister will like it.

From the oddments of cloth, cut out double-pages measuring 20 inches long by 10 inches wide (see Fig. 1), although these measurements may, of course, be varied to suit the material you have to hand. Do not attempt to make a thick book. Eight or ten pages are quite sufficient.

The edges of the pages may have V-shaped cuts made in them, as shown in Fig. 1. This will help to prevent the edges of the pages from fraying when in use.

If the cloth is too creased it is quite a good idea to pass a hot iron over it before securing the pages to each other. When you are satisfied with the condition of the pages they may be sewn together with two large stitches down the folded centre, as shown at Fig. 2. First, pass the needle up through the centre, at " A," down through " B," then along the centre fold to " C," and finally down through " A " again. Pull the stitches tight and tie off the two ends of the thread.

Your rag book is now ready to receive

Fig. 1

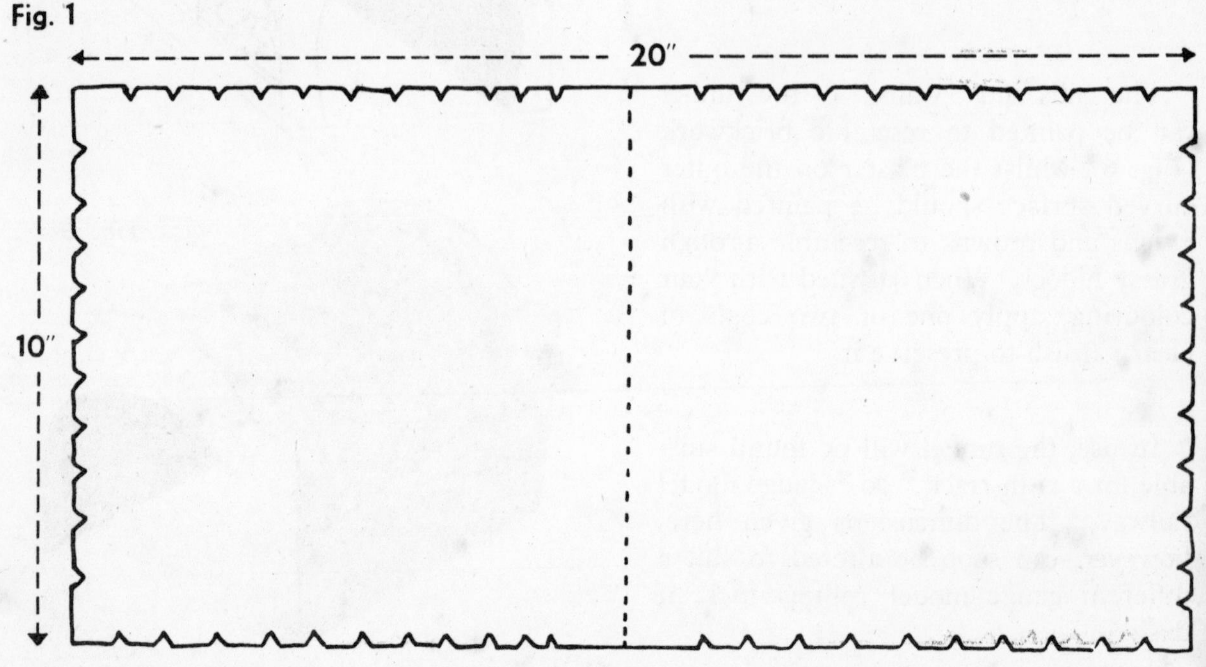

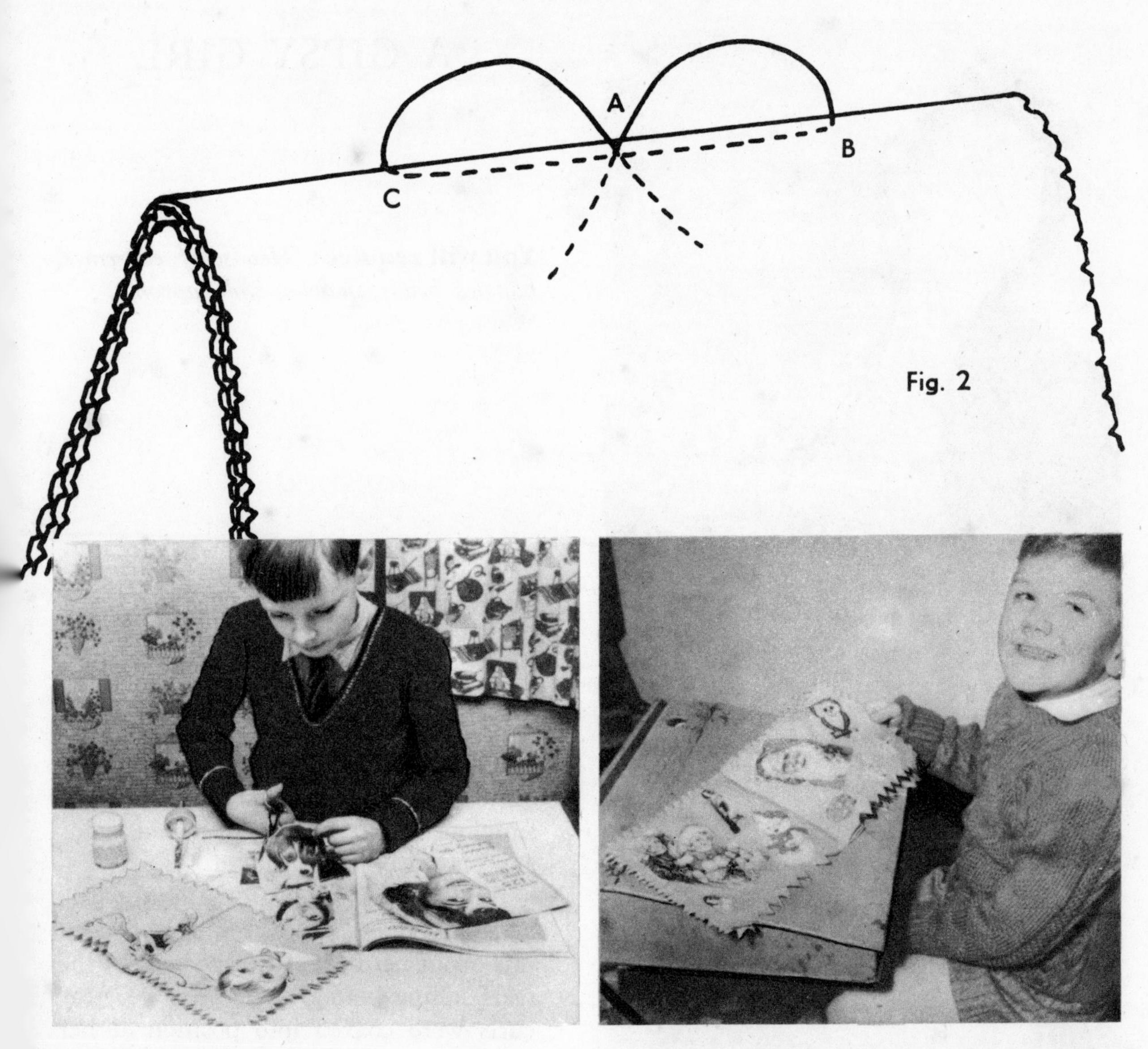

its illustrations. Collect all the old magazines and picture books that you can find. You will be surprised at the number of coloured pictures that you are able to glean from them. Make sure that you choose only those pictures most likely to interest the young owner of the rag book.

Having cut out the illustrations some care should be taken in arranging them in the most suitable positions. Try to have each page looking gay and interesting, but " different " from all the other pages.

Use a good paste or gum to stick the coloured cut-outs to the cloth pages. Make sure that you do not leave any surplus paste, either on the pictures or the pages, for fear of having the pages, themselves, stuck together.

I am sure that you will be really thrilled when you finally hand over the completed book to its young owner and see how happy he is with it.

A GIPSY GIRL

You will require: *Headscarf, ear-rings, bangles, beads, shawl or stole, apron.*

YOU must all know what fun there is in dressing-up—either for a fancy-dress party or just to lend point to a game.

Pauline decided to become a gipsy girl for a couple of tricks she wanted to try out on the others. She found it a fairly simple costume to produce from odds and ends around the house.

First, she picked the brightest silk headscarf that she could find. She tied this about her head, with the ends of the scarf falling behind. One or two stray curls were coaxed into position at her temples and about her ears.

For ear-rings she could have used large brass curtain-rings, secured about her ears with loops of thread, but, instead, decided in favour of some large Indian-style bangles looped around ordinary ear-rings.

Mother lent her a lacy, black stole and she wore her own charm bracelet and apron. As you can see by the illustration, a bunch of flowers completed the costume.

THE NOSEY MATCH-BOX

You will require :
One match-box.

HERE is a good way of starting up some party fun. It is just the sort of game to get everyone laughing.

All you need is the case from an empty match-box.

Stand your guests round in a circle and place the match-box on the end of your nose. You will find that with a slight push it will clip itself quite securely to your nose.

And now comes the fun. The person standing on your immediate right must take the match-box from you—but he or she must only use their nose!

Our illustration shows Robert and Stephen having a session at the game. Unfortunately, young Stephen has only a small nose and he has the greatest difficulty in removing the match-box from Robert.

Should the match-box be dropped by the person who is trying to take over, then he or she has to step out of the game. And so on, until there are only two people remaining. The winner is the one who survives this last duel.

If there are a great number of guests it is quite good fun to have two circles of people, with a match-box for each. They start at a given signal and the winning circle are those who complete the circuit first.

CLUB NOTEPAPER

You will require : *Blotting-paper, ink, brush, notepaper.*

HOW would you like to have some nicely printed notepaper for your club ? It is a simple-enough matter and with care and neatness it is possible to make quite a professional-looking little job of it.

You must first draw the outline of a suitable crest. If you cannot draw very well, try tracing something from an old book or comic. When you are satisfied with your crest, transfer the outline to a piece of blotting-paper. Use sharp scissors to cut out the crest. (Fig. 1.)

Gum the crest to a small piece of card. (Fig. 2.) Make quite sure that all parts of the blotting-paper cut-out, particularly the edges, are gummed securely to the card.

Fig 1

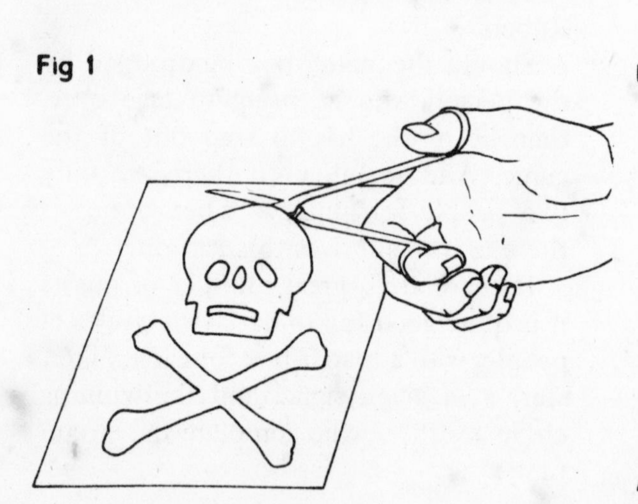

Fig 2

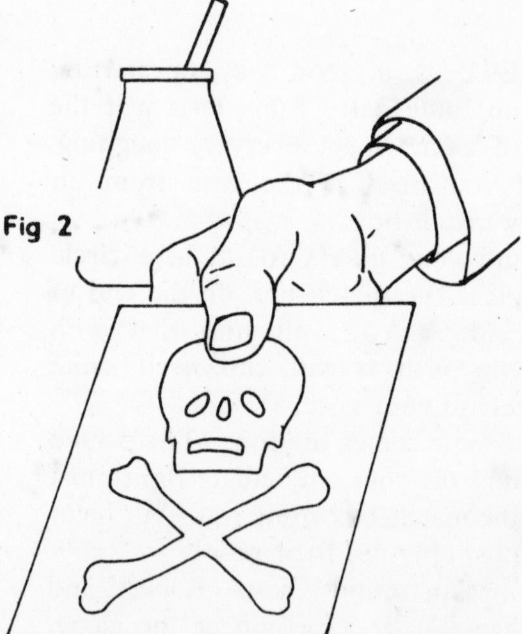

Now use a soft brush to " paint " the blotting-paper crest with ink. Take care that no ink is allowed to appear upon the card mount. (Fig. 3.) Any coloured ink may be used.

Place the painted crest face down on a sheet of plain notepaper. Do not let the painted cut-out move once it has touched the paper, otherwise a smudged print may result. It is also a good plan to have three or four thicknesses of newspaper lying perfectly flat beneath the notepaper. Once the crest has been correctly positioned, press down firmly with the heel of your hand, as shown in Fig. 4. Make sure that pressure is applied all over the back of the cut-out. Should you be unable to obtain sufficient pressure with your hand to obtain a clear print, place the notepaper and inked cut-out between the pages of a thick book and stand with your full weight upon the cover.

When you lift the mounted cut-out from the notepaper you should find a clear print has been made. (Fig. 5.) Should some parts of your crest have failed to print, this can usually be traced to the fact that insufficient pressure has been applied to these parts, or that too little ink has been brushed on the cut-out. On the other hand, if the edges of your print seem to have spread outwards, with unsightly blotching, this is probably caused by too much ink having been applied to the crest.

After one or two trial-and-error prints you should soon be producing some attractively headed notepaper.

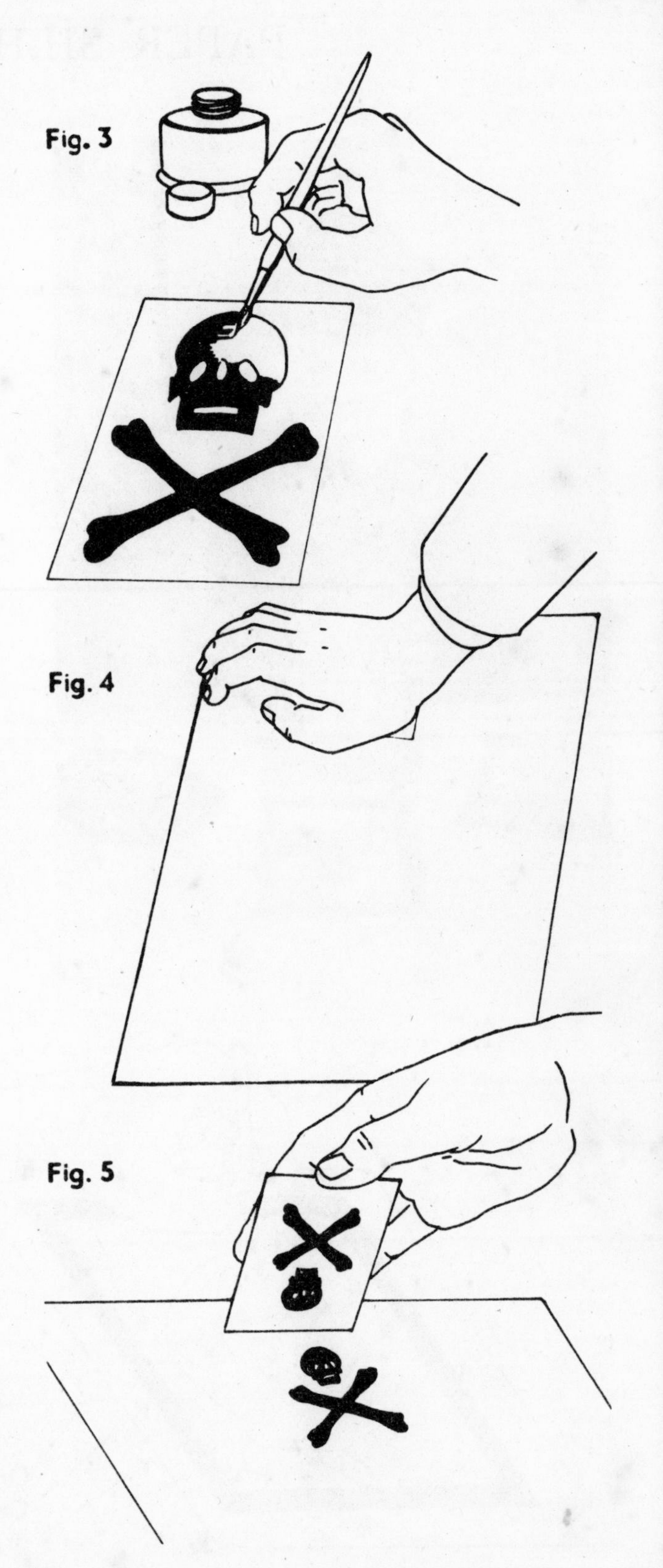
Fig. 3

Fig. 4

Fig. 5

PAPER SILHOUETTES

You will require : *White paper, coloured paper, pencil, carbon paper, scissors, gum.*

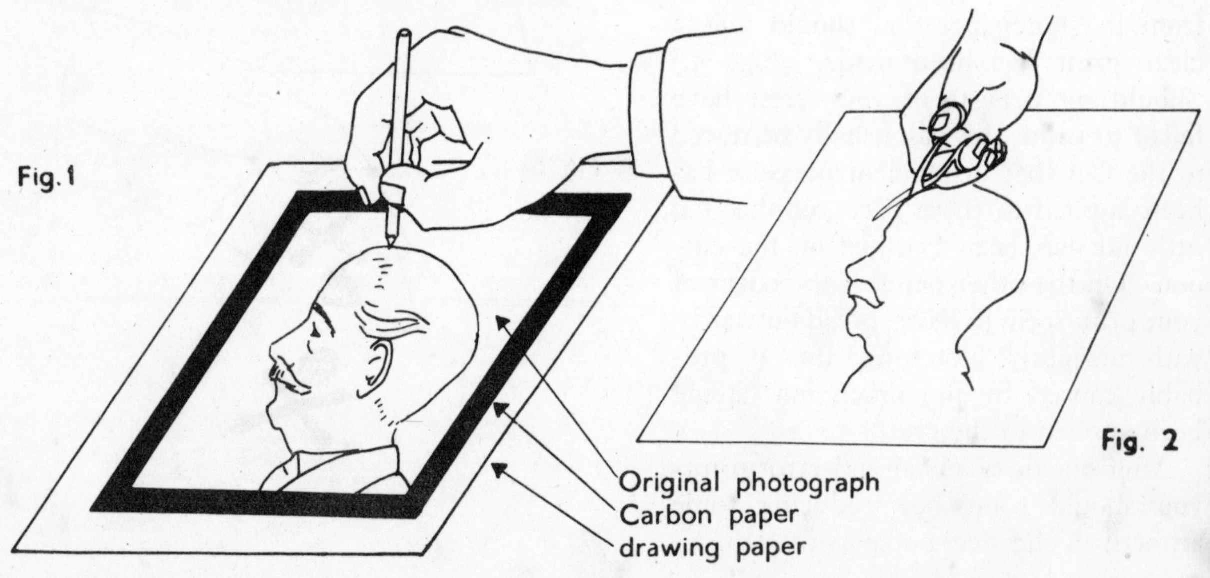

PHOTOGRAPHS of friends, relatives, famous people can all be used to provide the outlines for attractive silhouettes. Either real photographs or newspaper and magazine illustrations may be used. Profiles are best.

Place the original photograph on a sheet of carbon paper. Make sure that the latter has the carbon side face down on a sheet of white or coloured drawing-paper. With an HB pencil draw carefully round the outline of the features in the original. Press firmly with the pencil so that the carbon paper can transfer the outline to the drawing-paper beneath it. (Fig. 1.)

Remove the carbon paper and the original illustration. Use a small pair of sharp scissors to cut round the outline of your silhouette. (Fig. 2.)

The silhouette is then gummed to a sheet of paper of contrasting colour. Make sure that there is no surplus gum on the mounting-paper, and then place your silhouette between the pages of a thick book until the gum has dried. (Fig. 3.)

You will find that it is also an easy matter to provide your silhouette with a neat frame. Obtain a rectangle of mount paper—either white or coloured—that is an inch or so longer and wider than the mounting on which your silhouette is gummed. Fold this larger sheet of paper into quarters and cut the edges into an attractive shape, as shown by the smaller illustration in Fig. 4.

Open the larger sheet of paper and you will find the complete outer edge is decorated. The mount paper, on which your silhouette has already been gummed, should now be positioned centrally on the frame and secured there.

When you have tried your hand at cutting a few simple profile silhouettes, attempt something harder. The photograph shows some more difficult work which has been done. Stained-glass window effects look particularly attractive, especially if sections of the mount paper are painted to simulate stained glass.

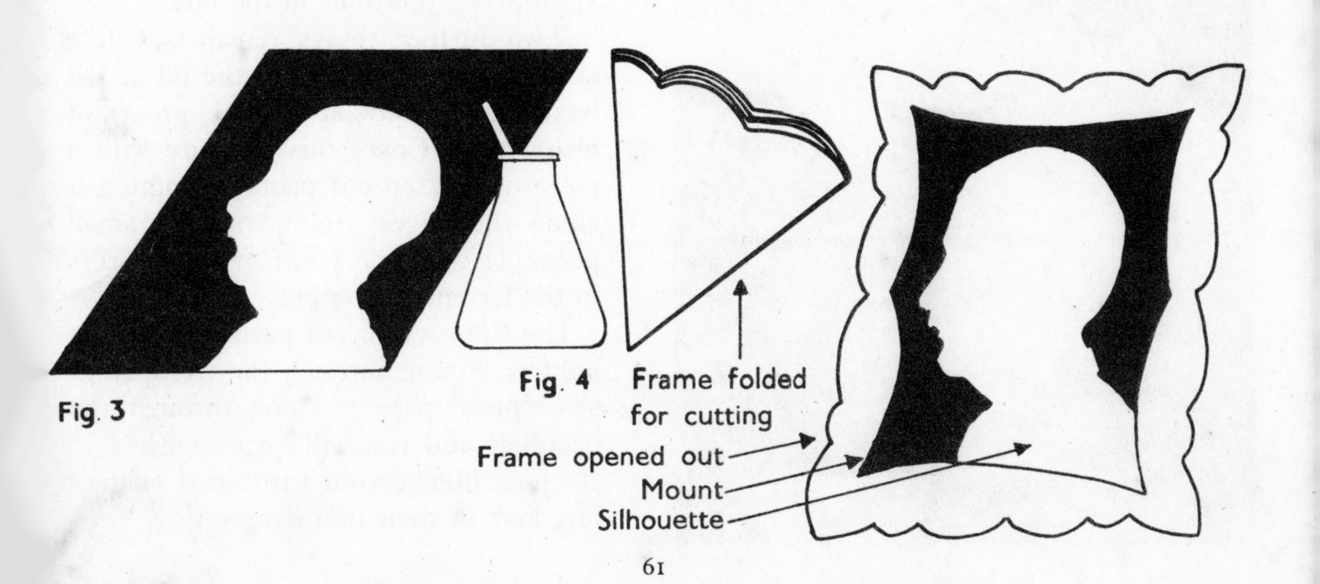

Fig. 3

Fig. 4

PEEPSHOW

You will require : *Shoe-box, comics, scissors, paints or crayons, cardboard, gum, greaseproof paper.*

TRY putting some favourite characters from your comics into a shoebox peepshow. You will need a hero plus the friends and foes taking part in that particular story. Look through your comics until you find something suitable, and then, like young Stephen, cut the various pictures out.

Mount the pictures on thin cardboard, leaving room for a small tab at the foot of each character. Cut the players out and bend these tabs over so that your characters will stand upright.

Your peepshow must now be given some suitable scenery. This may either be painted or crayoned directly to the inside of the box, or it may first be drawn up and coloured on drawing-paper and then gummed into position. With the scenery completed, gum the tabs at the feet of the characters and secure them in appropriate positions in the box.

Two further things remain : Cut a large square of card from the lid of the box, immediately above the group of characters. Cover this aperture with a piece of greaseproof paper, gumming it along the edges. Now make a small peephole with the point of the scissors in the far end of the box.

Hold the completed peepshow so that light is shining through the transparent greaseproof paper. Look through the peephole and you will be astonished to see how lifelike your cardboard characters look in their dramatic setting.

THE HUNGRY BOTTLE

You will require : *Milk bottle, hard-boiled egg, paper, match.*

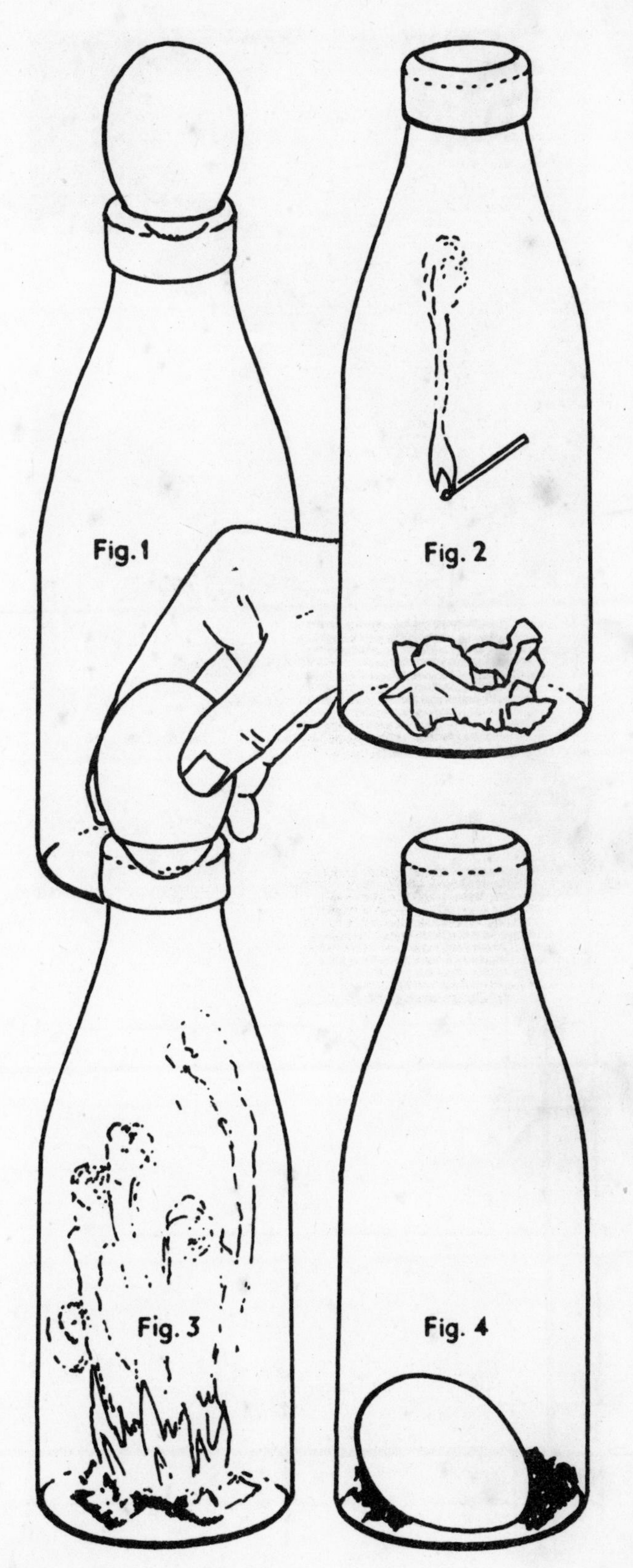

ASK Mother if she can spare a hard-boiled egg. Tell her that it is all in the cause of Science ! Remove the shell from the egg and show your friends that when placed in the mouth of a pint milk bottle the egg is considerably larger than the opening. (Fig. 1.)

Tell your friends that you can make the bottle so hungry that it will swallow the egg—before their very eyes ! Make sure that the inside of the bottle is perfectly dry. Place a screwed-up piece of paper inside the bottle and then drop a lighted match on to the paper. (Fig. 2.)

Directly the paper has caught alight, press the egg firmly into the mouth of the bottle and hold it there, as shown in Fig. 3. After a few seconds the flame inside the bottle will go out and you can release the egg.

Now that flame has used up all the oxygen inside the bottle and the outer air will try its hardest to enter the bottle. To your friend's astonishment, the outer air will exert such pressure that it will force the egg right into the bottle, giving every appearance that the bottle, itself, has actually swallowed the egg. (Fig. 4.)

LETTER RACK

You will require: *Plywood, cane, wooden beads, drill, saw, glue.*

You will need a piece of three-ply wood for the base of the letter rack. Cut this to measure 5 inches long by $1\frac{3}{4}$ inches wide. Round the four corners off with the aid of a file, and glasspaper the freshly sawn edges until they are perfectly smooth.

Mark out the positions for the nine holes shown from " A " to " F " in Fig. 1. Drill the holes right through the base with a $\frac{1}{8}$-inch drill.

Fig. 1

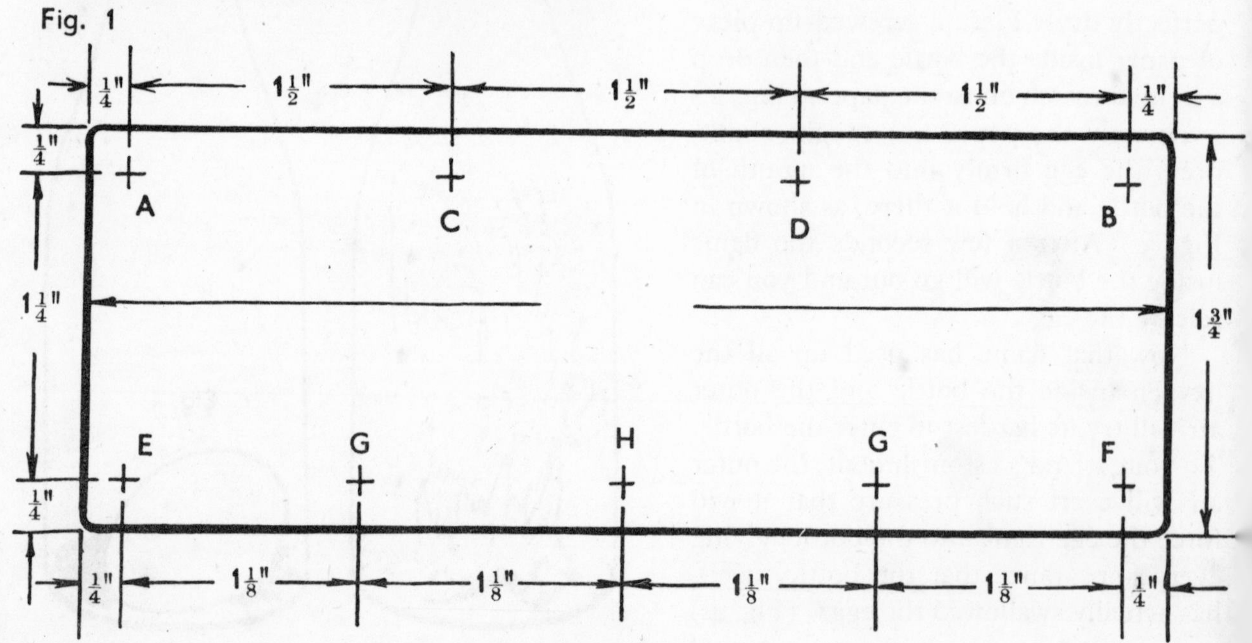

Buy a few lengths of Size 8 cane from a handicraft stockist's. Cut two pieces of cane, one measuring 11 inches long and the other 5 inches long. Soak them in water for a minute to make them pliable. The longer piece of cane must fit into the holes marked "A" and "D." Glue the cane into this position, with the two ends projecting sufficiently on the underside of the base to receive two beads, as shown in Fig. 2. Glue the wooden beads, obtainable at a handicraft shop, to the ends of the cane so that they form gay little feet for the letter rack.

The smaller length of cane should be bent to form an even curve, with its ends glued into the holes at "B" and "C."

Fig. 2

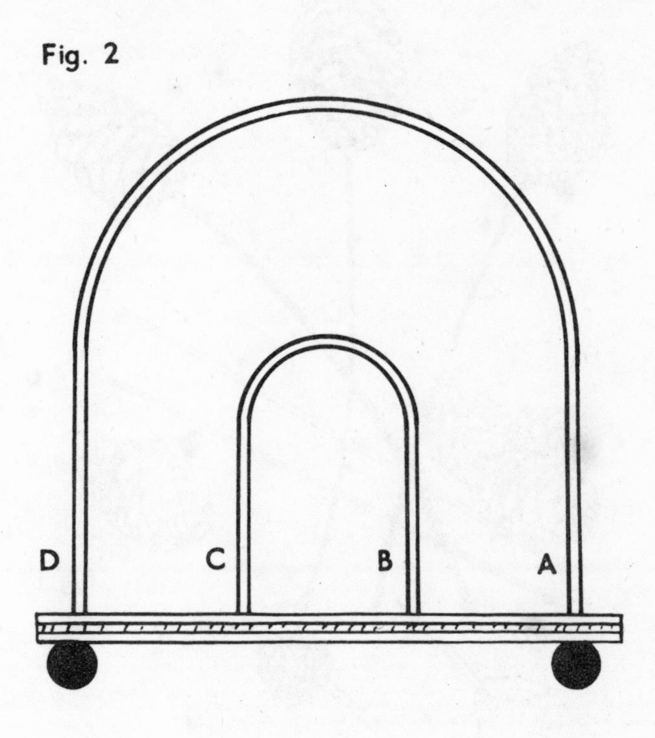

Four lengths of cane are required for the front of the rack. The longest piece should measure about 8 inches in length. It is glued into position in holes "E" and "F" and also has beads attached to its ends on the underside of the base.

Fig. 3

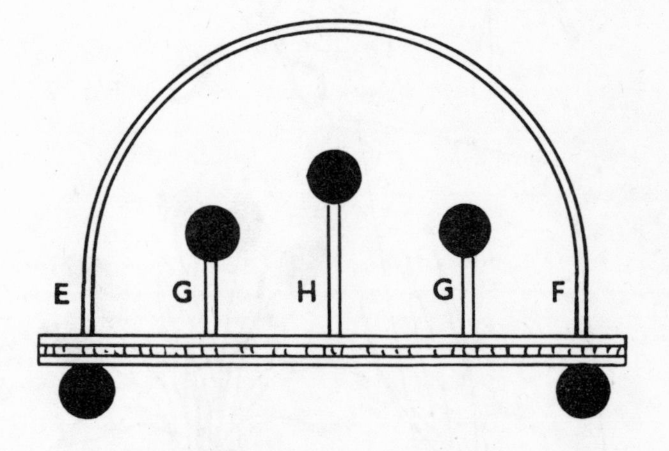

The remaining three pieces of cane for the front of the rack are quite short. These are glued into the holes "G" and "H" as shown in Fig. 3. The centre cane in hole "H" is $1\frac{1}{2}$ inches long and the two outer pieces in holes "G" are 1 inch long. These three pieces of cane have coloured wooden bead glued to their tops. (Fig. 3.)

The illustration shows the letter rack in use. It can be stood upon a convenient shelf or table, or will hang handily from a wall.

PINE-CONE POSIES

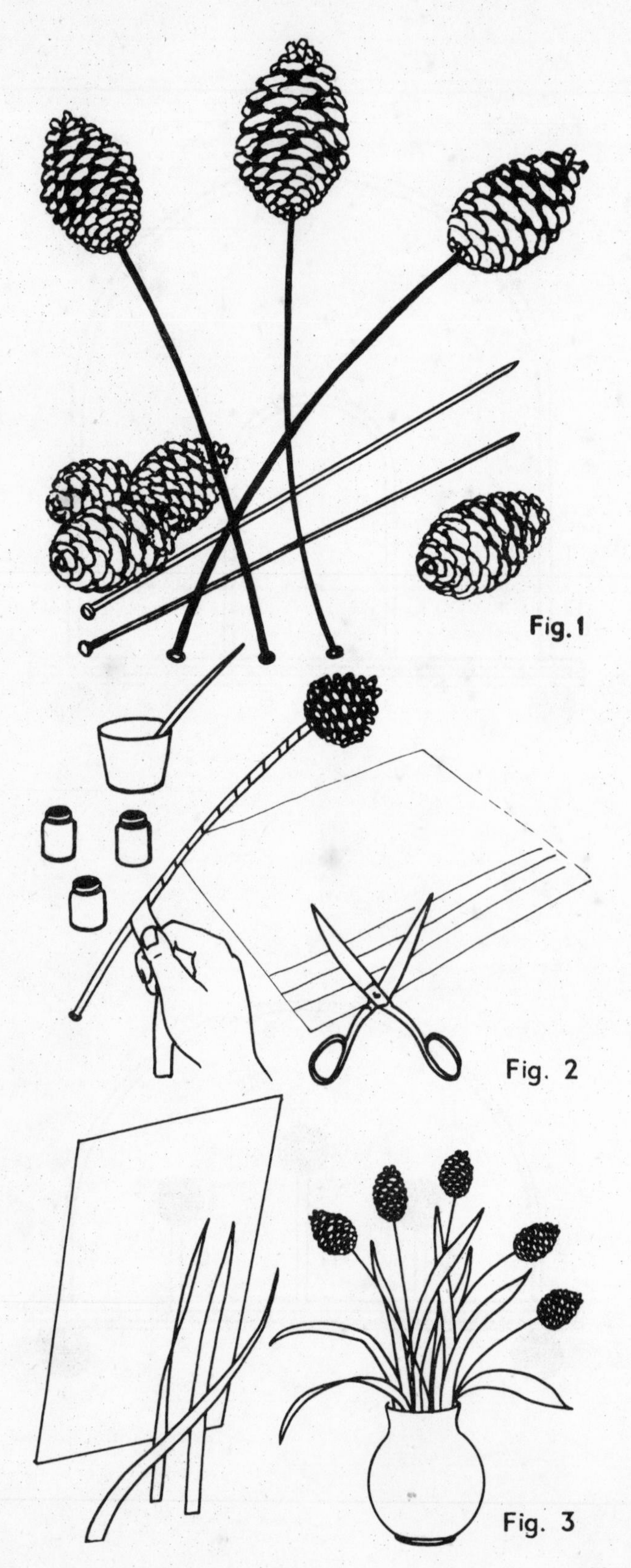
Fig. 1

Fig. 2

Fig. 3

You will require : *Pine-cones, knitting-needles, paints, green crêpe-paper, glue.*

TAKE a walk in the woods in Autumn and you will most probably gather a rich harvest of pine-cones of various shapes and sizes. Save the better specimens. Pine-cone posies will help to brighten a corner of the home during the dark days of winter.

Now collect some old knitting-needles. These are to serve as the stalks for your pine-cone flowers. Dip the sharp ends of the needles into glue and then impale the pine-cones on them. (Fig. 1.) Some of the needles should be slightly curved in the manner of true stalks.

Use brightly coloured enamels to paint the cones. Put them aside carefully until the enamel has dried. Next, cut some green crêpe-paper into thin strips, each about $\frac{1}{2}$ inch wide. Put a dab of glue on one end of these strips. Begin from this end, binding the paper round and round the knitting-needles. Glue the ends down and cut off any surplus paper. (Fig. 2.)

From the same crêpe-paper, cut several long, spear-shaped leaves. These should be an inch or so shorter than the flowers. Glue two or three leaves to the base of each stalk. Arrange your pine-cone posy in a suitable vase and there you have a gay, seasonal decoration. (Fig. 3).

SMOKE PATTERNS

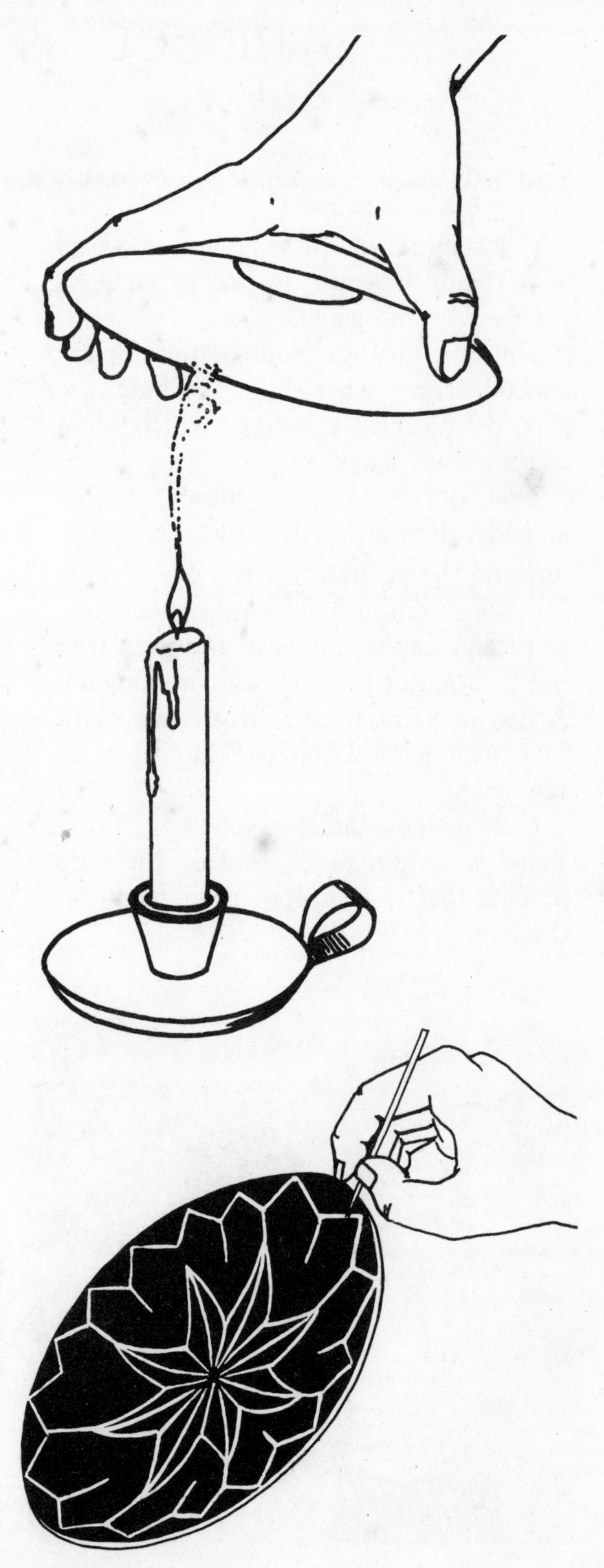

You will require: *Saucer, candles, matches, sharpened cane.*

YOU have no doubt heard of Indians sending up smoke signals, and perhaps have seen a smoker puffing smoke rings from his cigarette? Well, here is your chance to create attractive patterns from smoke.

But you will not need a bonfire, nor a cigarette. Put a match to the wick of a candle, instead. Then hold a small plate or a saucer just above the flame so that a deposit of carbon is left on the underside by the candle flame.

Move the saucer or plate around so that it receives an even coating of carbon all over. But take care not to burn yourself.

When the saucer is completely coated on one side, take a piece of sharpened cane and commence to scratch your pattern on the coating of carbon. The cane will remove the deposit, leaving the white chinaware showing through. Should you make a mistake, place that part of the saucer over the candle flame until it is again covered with carbon.

The diagram shows a simple type of pattern that can be made in the "smoke." You will find it a matter of practice before being able to produce some really exquisite patterns from smoke.

THE "GUESS WHO" GAME

You will require: *Large paper bags, scissors, paints and brush.*

ANY time you have a gathering of friends do not forget to have a " Guess Who " game.

The main things required for this are several large paper bags. These are turned into head coverings which serve as humorous disguises.

One of the first essentials, before actually decorating the bags, is to determine the position for the eyes. This is easily accomplished by asking someone to place a bag on his head and indicatng the position of his eyes with his fingers. A dab of paint from a brush will mark this position and the bag can then be removed.

Cut small eye-holes in the bag. Their shape can often be decided by the type of face that it is proposed to paint on the bag.

For this particular game of " Guess Who," the " gang " had decided to choose animal faces for their disguises. There was a great deal of fun and merriment as they hunted through annuals and comics for suitable animal faces to copy on their bags.

Picture shows Pauline putting the finishing touches to a panda disguise. She is cutting away the top of the paper bag to form the ears. It is not always necessary to cut the bag in this way. Sometimes the corners can be folded and gummed down to form ears. Or the bag can be left at its full size, especially if long ears or antlers are required.

When all the disguises had been completed, the game began. A cord was stretched across one half of the room and a sheet was suspended over it.

Charmaine elected to be the first "guesser." She went out of the room while the others quickly changed their disguises around and put them on. When Charmaine returned she found a row of comical heads appearing above the top of the sheet.

Every paper-bag disguise had a pair of laughing eyes, but Charmaine was not very successful in guessing their rightful owners. Pictures show how perplexed she was, and also shows how difficult was her task. Before looking at the last illustration can you guess who is hiding under each paper bag?

As you can see Charmaine had a surprise when the disguises were removed. Did you succeed in guessing who was hiding under those paper bags?

YACHT BOOK-ENDS

You will require : *Wood, cane, paper, putty, screws, paint, brush, glue.*

HERE is a novel pair of book-ends to help keep your favourite books in order.

You will need four pieces of clean-grained wood, each measuring $4\frac{1}{2}$ inches long by $2\frac{1}{2}$ inches wide and $\frac{1}{2}$ inch thick. Saw two corners off each piece, as shown by the shaded areas in Fig. 1. Sandpaper the four pieces of timber until they are perfectly smooth on all sides and edges.

The side view of Fig. 1 illustrates how two sections of wood are assembled to form one book-end. The screws or nails used to join the two pieces of wood together should be driven well home so that their heads are slightly below the surface.

Figure 2 shows the actual size of the small vessels. The hulls can be whittled and filed from small blocks of wood (balsa wood makes the task an easy one). The masts and spars are fashioned from suitable lengths of thin cane or wire. The masts and the bowsprits should be glued into holes made in the hulls to receive them, as shown in the side view of Fig. 2.

The sails for your miniature yachts

Fig. 1

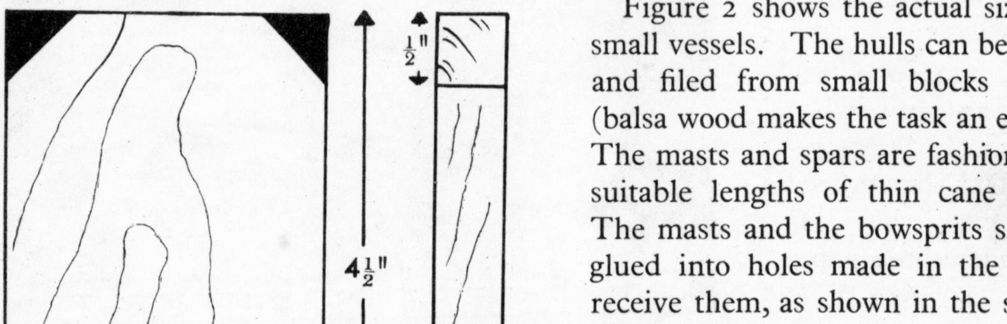

$2\frac{1}{2}''$

$4\frac{1}{2}''$

$\frac{1}{2}''$

4

$\frac{1}{2}''$

SIDE VIEW

are cut from white drawing-paper. Their exact shapes are shown in Fig. 3. Cut the sails out carefully and glue them into their positions on the masts and spars. The flag may be cut from coloured paper.

Next comes the task of providing your small vessels with a lifelike sea on which to sail. This is modelled from ordinary putty. But first, drive a nail or screw upwards from the underside of each book-end, so that its end protrudes for an inch above the surface of the wood. Spread some glue or oil-paint on the top of the book-ends and model your putty seas on this.

The projecting screw serves the dual purpose of holding the hull of the model yacht in position and helping to retain the putty sea.

Use your fingers to pinch the putty into imitation waves. At the same time, press the putty firmly against the wooden base of the book-end.

When the seas have been completely modelled to your satisfaction, gently press the hulls of the small ships into their required positions and engage them with the ends of the screws.

With the yachts now sailing their putty seas, it is best to put the book-ends on one side in a warm room to allow the putty to dry. Do not forget to cover the screw-heads with small quantities of putty, smoothing it flush with the surrounding surface of the wood.

Complete your book-ends by painting them with bright enamel paints. The woodwork can be any colour you choose, but try to paint the seas with realistic blues and greens, capped with white.

Paint the hulls of the miniature vessels, curve the sails and flags, and your book-ends are complete.

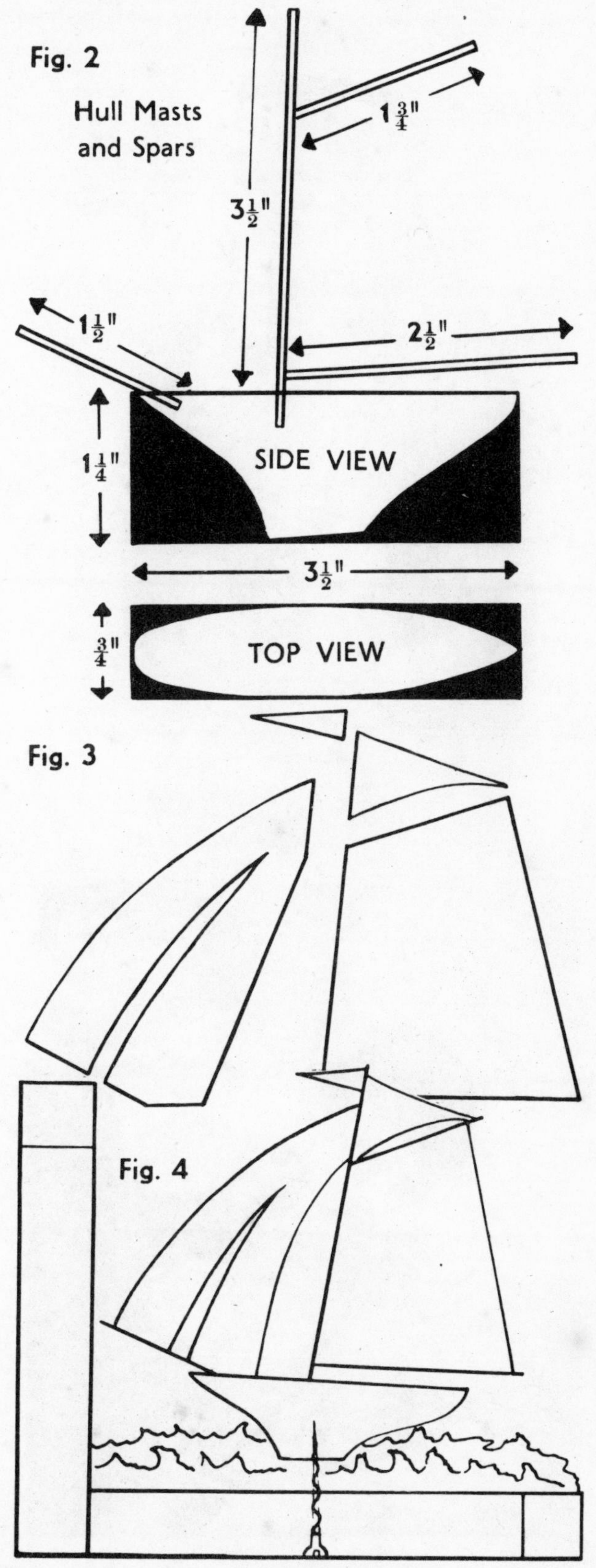

THE SHEIK OF ARABY

You will require : *Towel, tie, scarf, wooden or cardboard dagger, sandals or Wellington boots, and a burnt cork.*

MAY the sands of the desert never grow cold! Robert decided that he was finished with the Foreign Legion. Who ever heard of Legionnaires owning oil-wells and becoming rich men? No, for his next spell of dressing-up he decided he would rather be an Arabian sheik.

There are several ways of "growing" beards, moustaches, and side-burns.

One of the simplest, and certainly among the easiest to remove, is to use a burnt cork.

All that is required is to hold a cork in the flame of a candle for a few seconds until the end is charred. Allow this to cool, and you will find that you have an excellent means of drawing any facial adornments you may require.

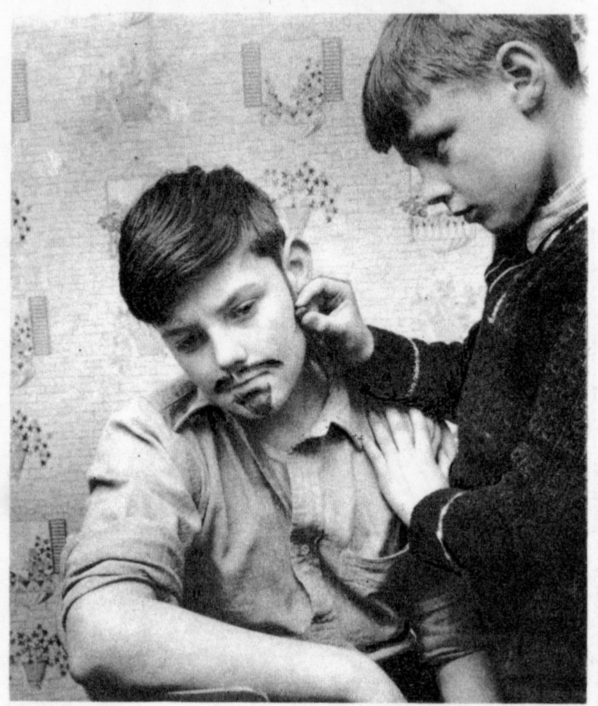

Here you can see Stephen at work on his brother. Robert looks quite fierce with those additions to his face, doesn't he?

A towel was tied about his head with an old neck-tie. His shirt pulled outside his trousers and belted in to his waist by a wide scarf. A painted cardboard dagger thrust into the scarf. Sandals or Wellington boots on his feet, and there we are. A costume good enough for any play or fancy-dress party.

MAKING A COLOURED WOOLLEN BALL

You will require : *Cardboard, scraps of coloured wool, darning-needle, scissors.*

VERY often, for games about the house, you require a really soft ball that can be thrown with plenty of force without being likely to cause any breakages in the home.

One of these simple woollen balls is just the thing. They can be made in really gay colours. They are large enough to grasp easily when throwing or catching, and they are soft enough to ensure that the windows, mirrors, and pictures will be quite safe.

Begin by cutting two discs of cardboard measuring about 4½ inches in diameter. From the centre of each disc remove two circular pieces about 1½ inches in diameter. Place both rings of card together and commence binding scraps of coloured wool around them. Use three or four strands of wool at a time when binding so that you complete the ball quickly. (Fig. 1.)

Carry on binding wool around the cardboard rings until you have to use a darning-needle to pass the last few strands of wool through the centre. When the wool is tightly packed around the cardboard, take a pair of scissors and cut round the edge of the ball, taking care that the scissors cut exactly between the two discs of cardboard.

When the wool has been carefully cut all round the edge, bind a strand of wool tightly two or three times round the centre of the ball, between the two pieces of cardboard. Slip the cardboard rings off, and there is your completed ball.

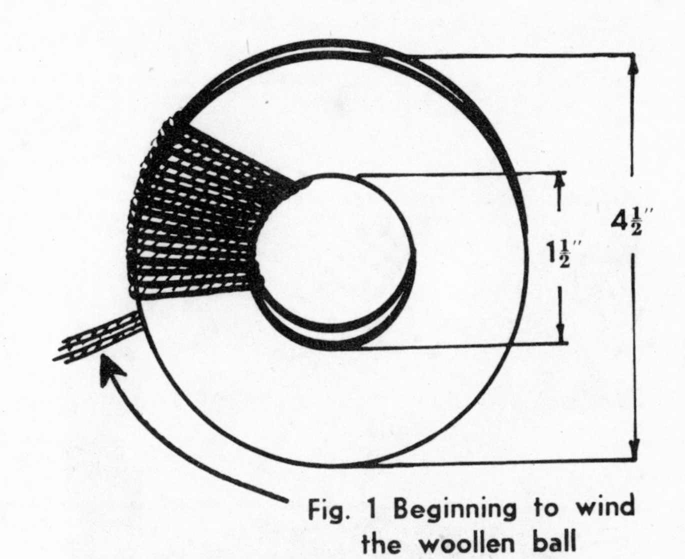

Fig. 1 Beginning to wind the woollen ball

PEN-NIB DARTS

You will require: *Old pen-nibs, hammer, paper, scissors.*

DO you throw your old pen-nibs away? They can be turned into very neat little darts. You will not require the actual points of the nib, they should be broken off, as shown in Fig. 1.

The ends of the nibs must now be split in order that they can receive paper flights. Two light blows with a hammer, first on the side and then on the flat of the nib, will cause the metal to split in a satisfactory manner. (Fig. 2.)

Flights for your darts are made from $2\frac{1}{2}$-inch squares of paper. They should be folded first in half, then in quarters, and finally in eighths, as shown in Fig. 3.

Reshape the paper flights so that they may be inserted into the split ends of the small darts. (Fig. 4.)

These darts may be used on an ordinary dart-board or can be employed in making up some original dart games. The photograph shows Terry and Robert engaged in a game of draught darts, using an old draughts-board as a target. Each player has three pen-nib darts. Robert's darts had white flights and Terry's had black flights. The player is only allowed to score a point when his dart lands in an opponent's square. The first player to reach a prearranged total score becomes the winner.

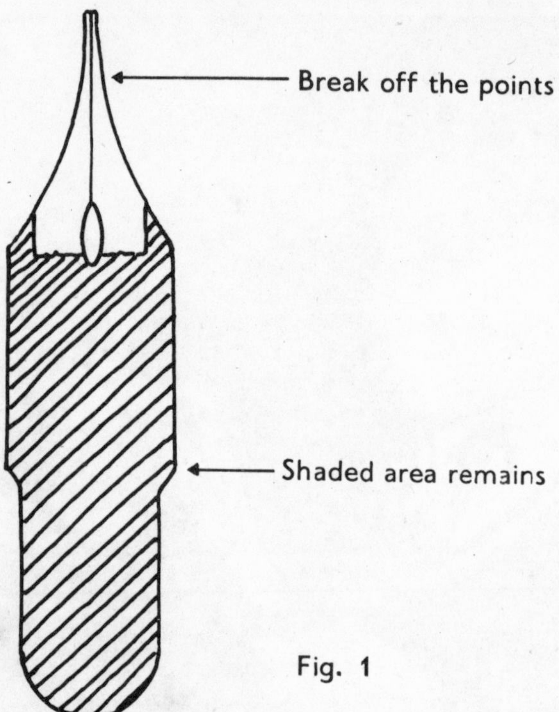

Fig. 1

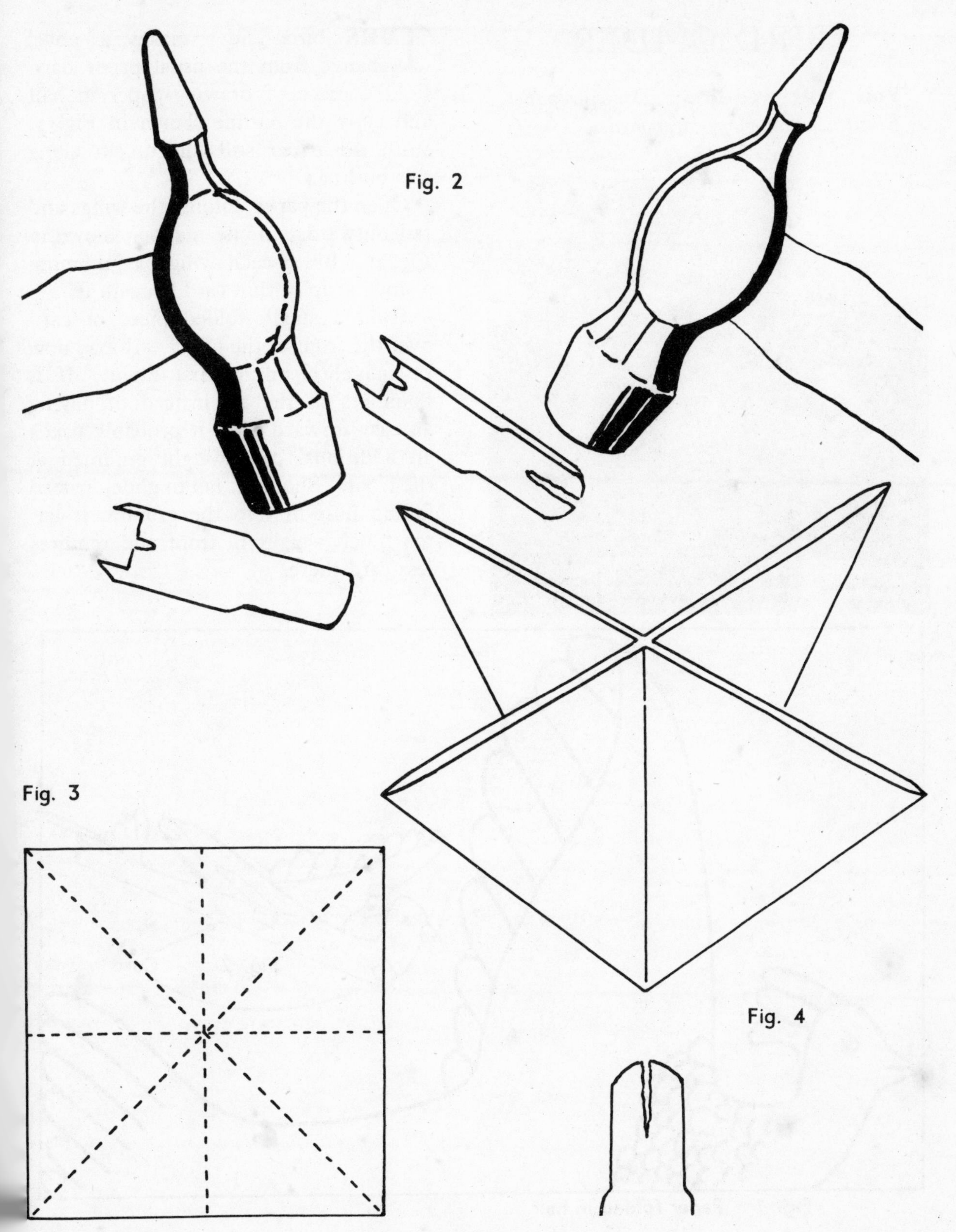
Fig. 2

Fig. 3

Fig. 4

BIRD GLIDER

You will require: *Drawing-paper, pencil, scissors, gum, cardboard.*

THIS bird glider makes a novel change from the usual paper dart. Fold a piece of drawing-paper in half and copy the outline shown in Fig. 1. With the paper still folded, cut along this outline.

Open the paper, folding the wings and tail outwards, in the manner shown in Fig. 2. Brace each wing by gumming a small strip of thin card beneath it.

Gum a small, folded piece of card over the front of the glider. It may now be launched on its first flight. If it flounders in the air instead of having an easy forward glide it probably needs an additional card weight gummed at the front. Should it fail to glide, instead falling nose-first to the ground, it has too much weight in front and requires less card there.

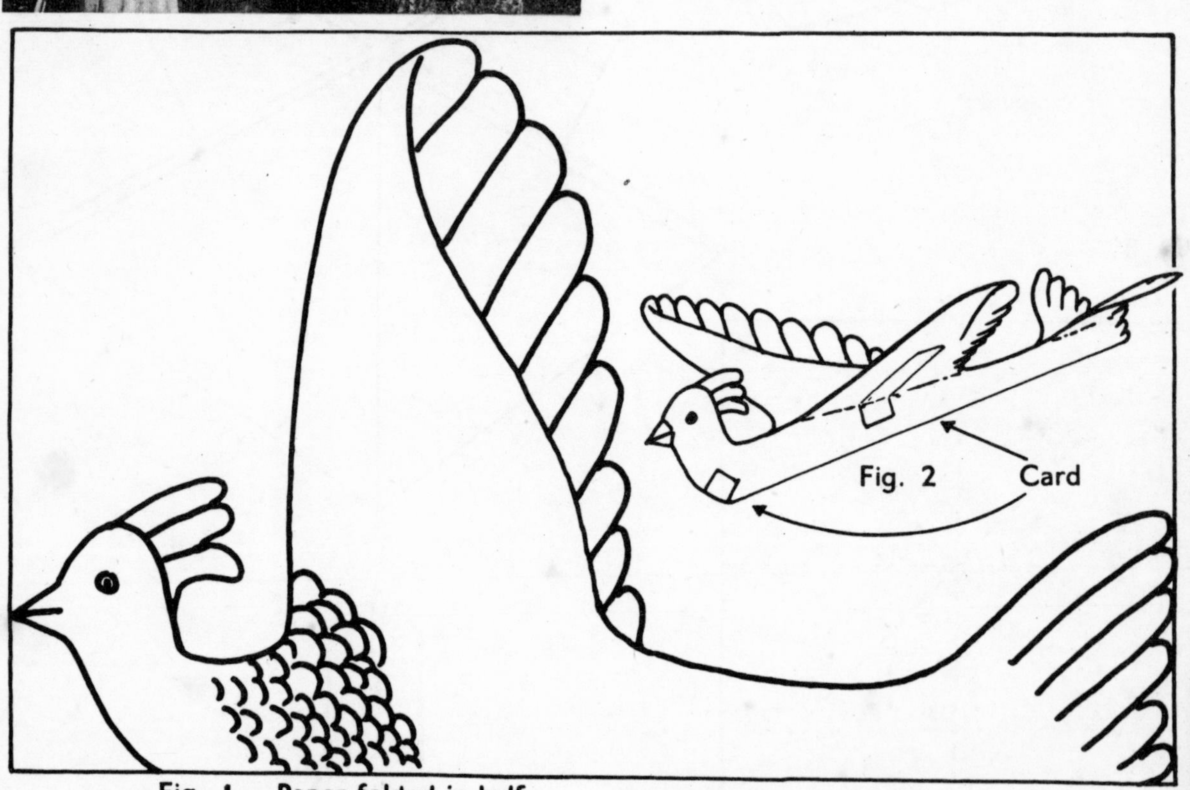

Fig. 1 Paper folded in half

A PAPER BANGER

Fig. 1. Fold along dotted lines.

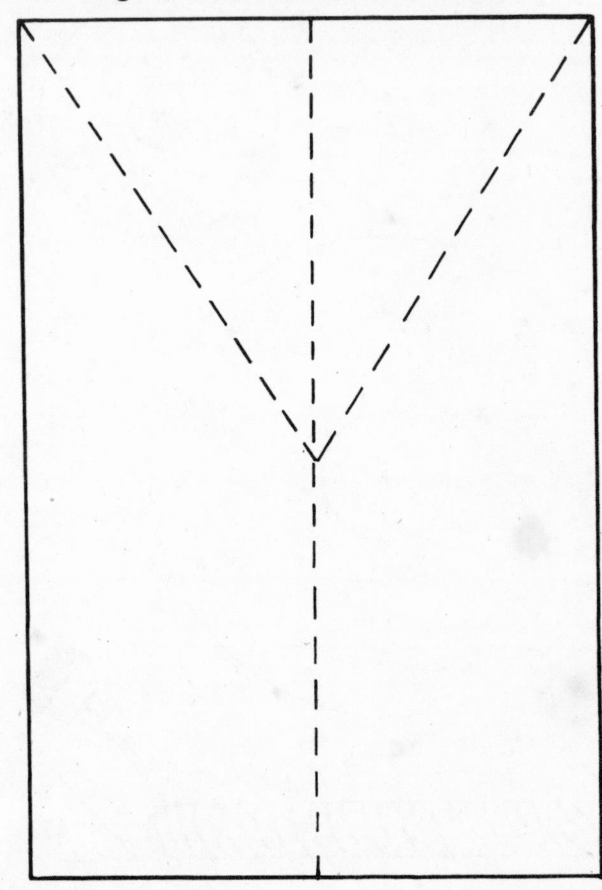

You will require: *Brown paper, scissors.*

ORDINARY brown wrapping-paper can be used to make a super banger.

Cut a sheet of strong brown paper into a rectangle measuring eight inches by seven inches. Fold this in half, across the width, and then fold one corner down to the unfolded edge.

Tuck this folded corner-piece down in the centre, as illustrated in Fig. 1. Grip the banger with finger and thumb on the unfolded corners. Raise the banger above your head and bring your arm down with a sudden movement. Air pressure will cause the folded triangular section to fly outwards with a most satisfactory report.

Picture shows Stephen demonstrating his paper banger to Pauline.

Fig. 1

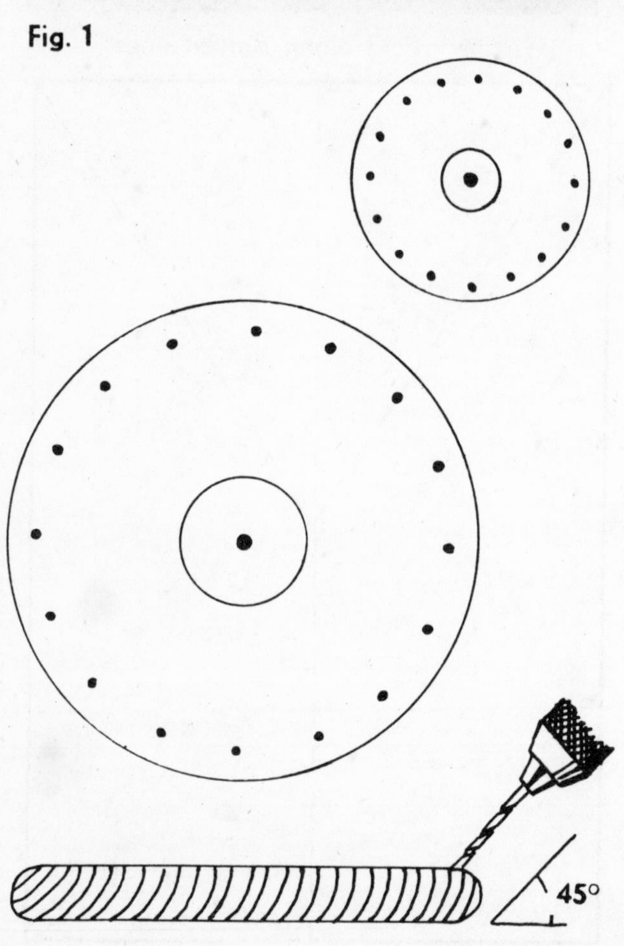

TOY-WHEEL TABLE LAMP

You will require : *Toy wheels, cane, drill, glue, electric fittings, screwdriver.*

TWO wooden toy wheels provide the top and base for this contemporary little table-lamp. The large wheel should be about 4 inches in diameter and the small wheel 2 inches in diameter. Mark the positions for sixteen holes around the edges of each wheel. (Fig. 1.) These should all be an equal distance apart. Use a $\frac{1}{8}$-inch drill and keep it at an angle of forty-five degrees, as shown in the smaller illustration at Fig. 1.

Screw a bulb-holder fitment (ask the shopkeeper for a bayonet-type holder) to the top of the small wheel. (Fig. 2.) Note that the holes should be on the underside of the wheel.

You will need sixteen pieces of No. 10 or 12 cane for the sides of the table lamp. Each piece should measure $5\frac{1}{2}$ inches in length and they should be glued into the holes around the edges of the two wheels, as shown in Fig 3.

Pass the end of an electric lead up through the small wheel and out via the bulb-holder. Unscrew the top of the holder, strip the insulation away from the two ends of the lead and connect them to the holder. (Let Father check this connection to make quite sure you have done it correctly.) (Fig. 4.)

Replace the top of the holder and attach a suitable plug to the free end of the lead. Instructions for making the shade are on the next page.

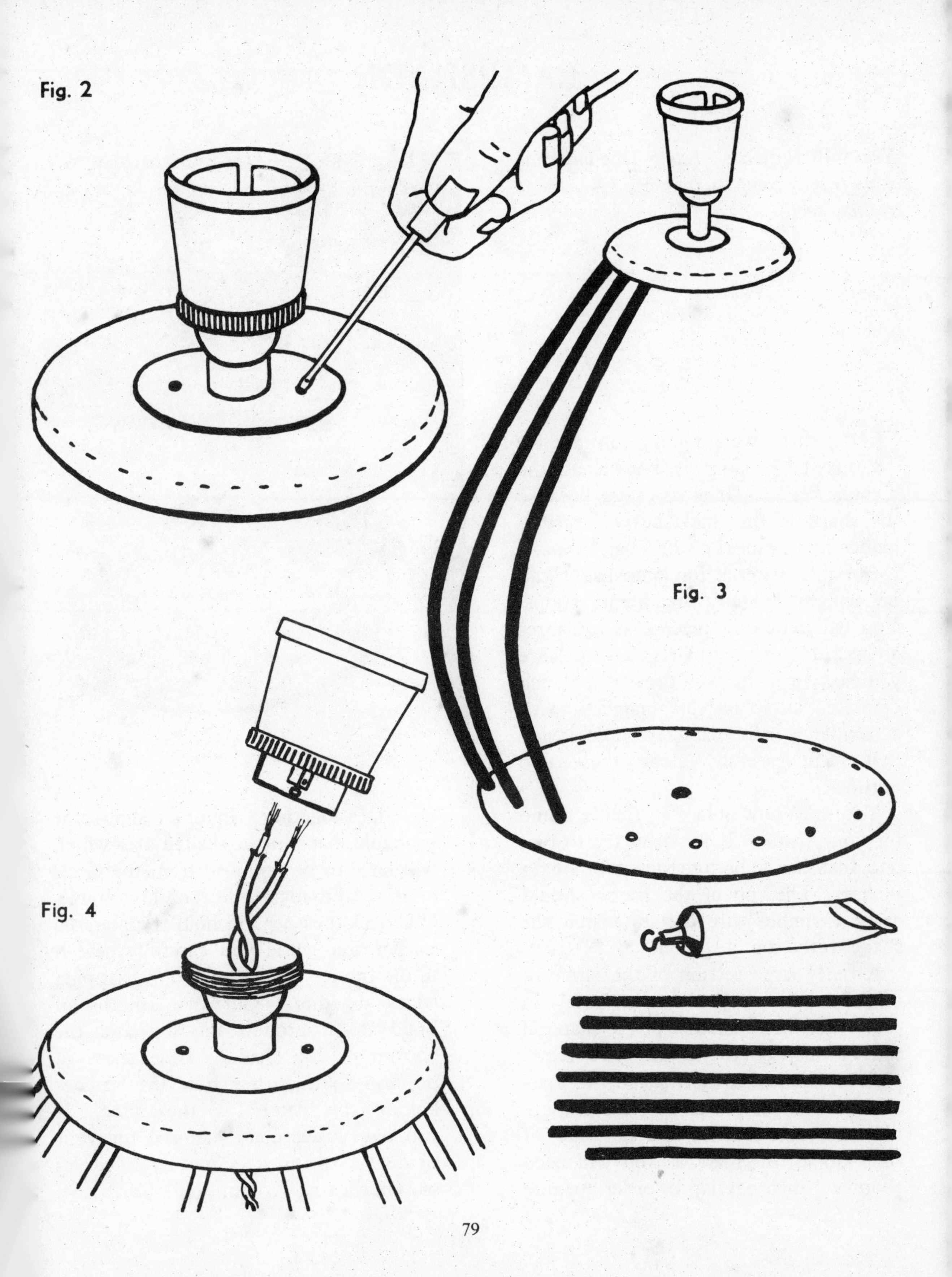
Fig. 2
Fig. 3
Fig. 4

LAMPSHADE

You will require : *Lampshade material, wire frame, compass, scissors, glue, braid, clothes-pegs.*

THE shade we are going to make for our table lamp is known as the " coolie " type. It is so called because the shape of the shade bears a resemblance to a Chinese coolie's hat.

Suitable material for lampshades can be bought at most handicraft shops. You will require a piece that measures at least 16 inches square. Use a large compass to help you draw a 16-inch diameter circle on this material, with a smaller 4-inch diameter circle inside that. Cut carefully along these two outlines.

You must now obtain a suitable frame for your shade. If possible, try to buy one that has a bottom diameter of 12 inches. The top of the frame should carry a simple wire clip to fasten the shade to the top of the bulb.

A fairly large section of the circle of material will need to be cut away in order that the remainder of the material can be shaped around the wire frame. Make a single cut first, shape the material around the frame, and mark where the cut edge comes. Do not cut off right up to this mark as you will need about a 1-inch overlap in order to glue the edges together. Figure 1 shows the probable shape in the shaded area which will have to be removed from the circle of material to make it fit round the frame.

Use clothes-pegs to hold the material in position while you carefully sew it to the frame. Glue the two overlapping edges together. Cut two lengths of braid to fit around the top and the bottom of the shade. Glue these in position so that they hide the stitches holding the material to the frame. If you have used plain material for your shade try painting some large circles of contrasting colour on the shade.

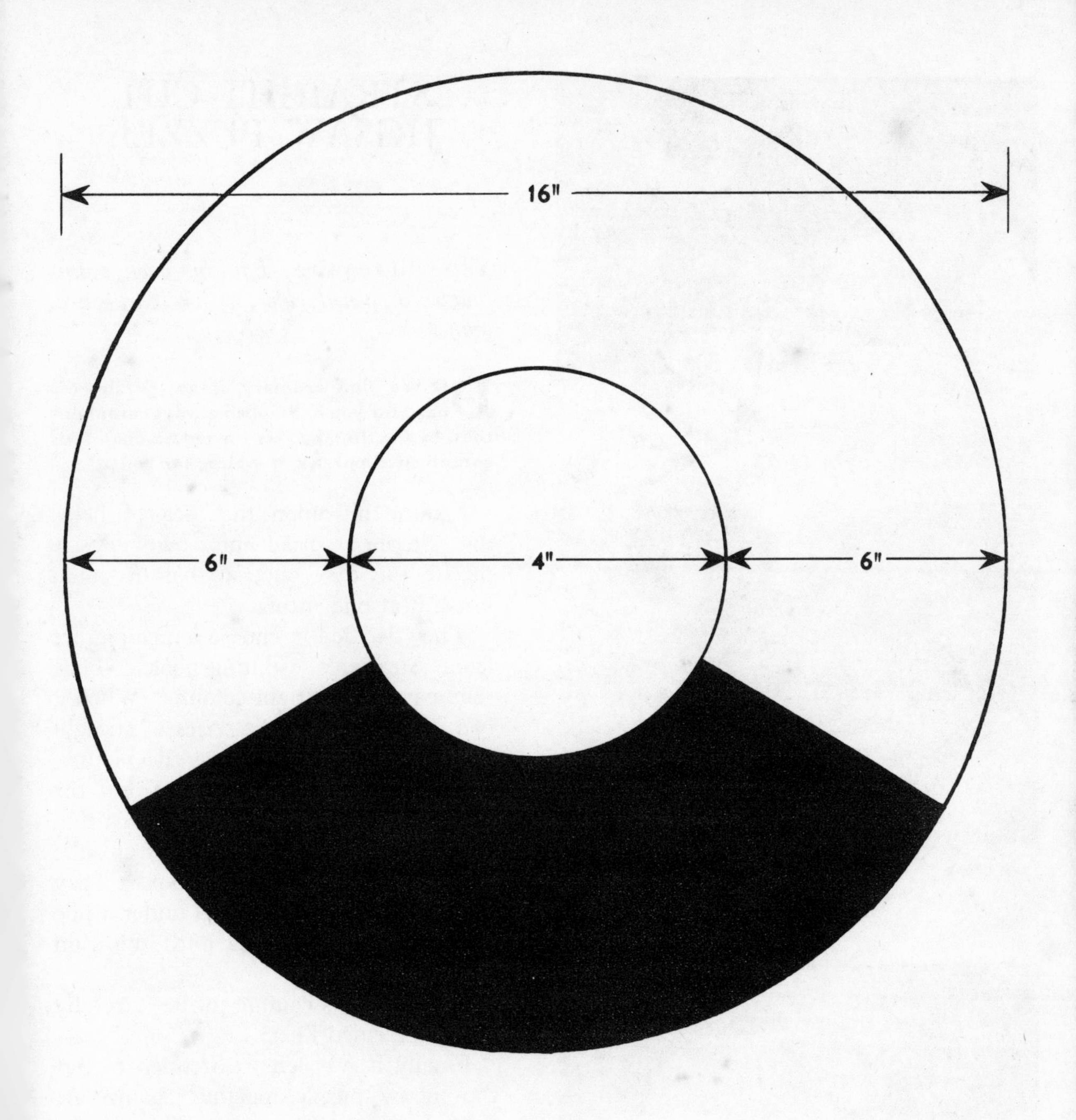
16"
6"
4"
6"

STRAIGHT-CUT JIGSAW PUZZLE

You will require: *Painting-book, paints and brush, pencil, ruler, scissors, cardboard, gum.*

DO you find ordinary jigsaw puzzles too hard for you? Stephen always complains that, by the time he gets started on one of his complicated puzzles, it is time for bed.

Pauline hit upon the idea of helping Stephen make his own jigsaw puzzle—an easy one, so that he could finish it at one sitting.

They decided to choose a nice picture from Stephen's painting-book. This, they painted in bright colours. When it had dried they ruled a series of straight lines both down and across the picture.

Having cut the picture from the painting-book, they gummed it to a thin piece of cardboard obtained from the side of a breakfast-cereal box. They placed the picture and card under a pile of telephone directories until the gum had dried.

Picture shows Pauline cutting carefully along the ruled lines.

Finally it was left to Stephen to put the jigsaw puzzle together again. At first, he thought it would prove too simple for him (after all, he is nine years old!) But, despite the large pieces and the straight cuts used to separate them, he found it passed an interesting fifteen minutes. And he knows that his painting-book has a lot more puzzles for him, when they have been coloured and cut out.

PENNY THROUGH A HALFPENNY

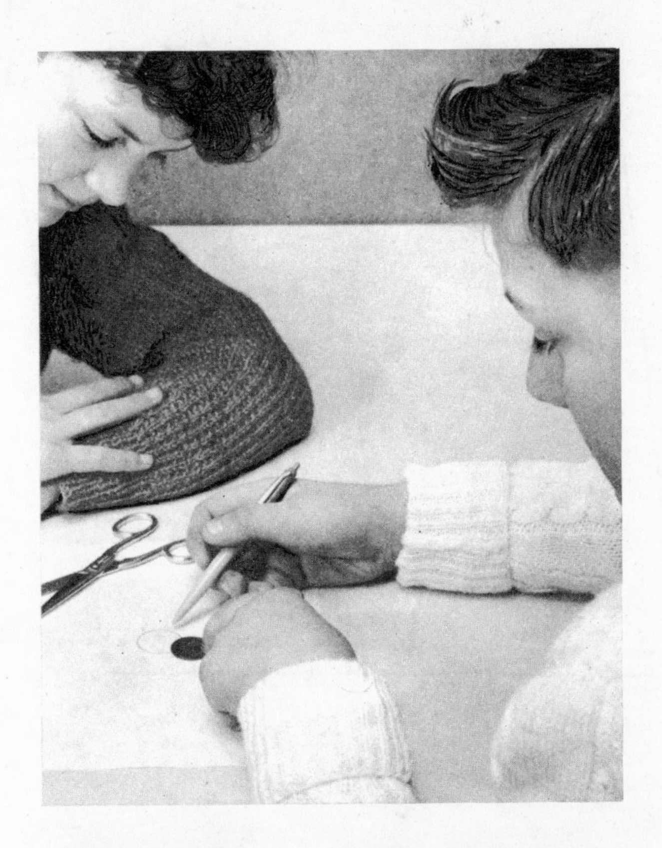

You will require : *Pencil, paper, scissors, halfpenny, penny.*

PAULINE had heard the saying about getting a quart into a pint pot. You may remember, earlier in this book, she had seen Robert pour a glass of water and a glass of cotton wool both into one tumbler. Even so, she found it difficult to accept when Robert told her that he could make a penny go through a hole only the size of a halfpenny.

First, she watched as he drew round a halfpenny, and noticed that when he cut this circle of paper out he cut slightly inside the line so that the hole was indeed the exact size of the coin.

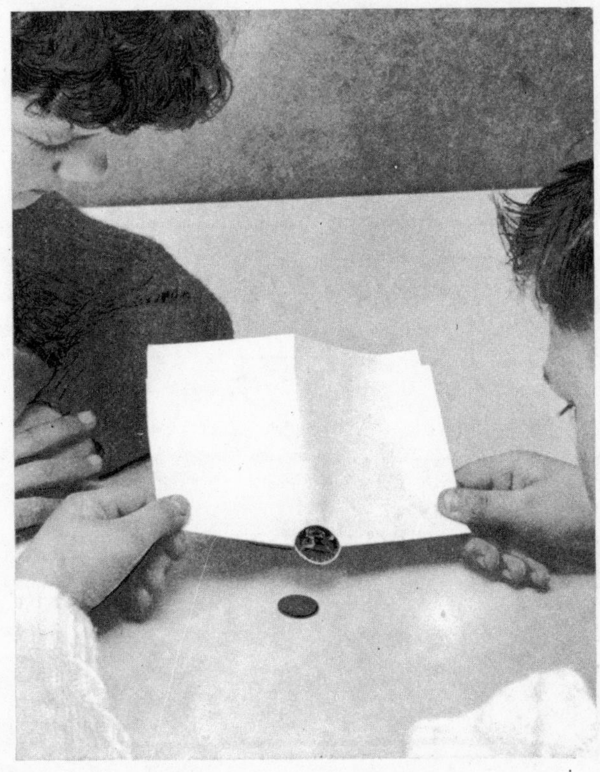

What she had not expected was to see him fold the paper in half, across the centre of the hole. He then slipped the penny down inside the folded paper. As he raised the ends of the paper, the hole widened and the penny slipped through. See if you can catch your friends with this trick.

MAKE A PARACHUTE

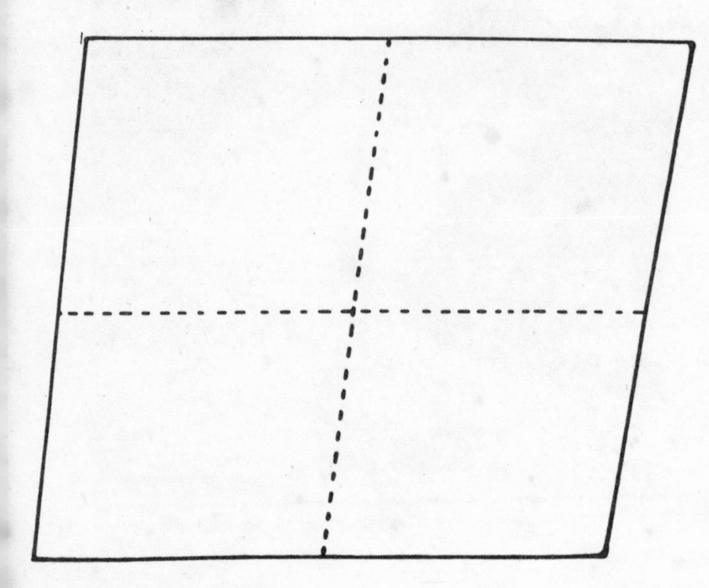

Fig. 1

Fig. 2

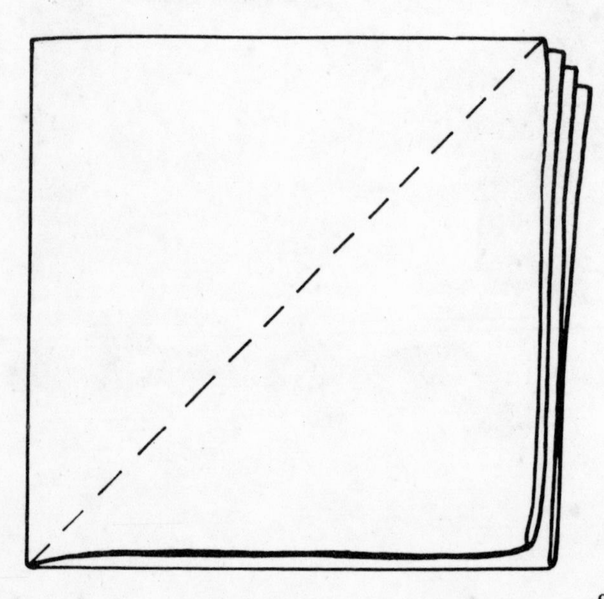

You will require : *Piece of silky material, scissors, twine, nut and bolt.*

TAKE a piece of silk or similar material that is about 18 to 20 inches square. Fold it first into halves and then into quarters, as shown in Fig. 1.

Fold it a third time, but from corner to corner, as illustrated in Fig. 2.

Fold again, as shown by the dotted line of Fig. 3. This fourth and last fold will give your small parachute sixteen panels.

Draw a circle with your compass or round the edge of a small jar, and then cut off the outer edges of the panels as shown in Fig. 4.

Stitch sixteen lengths of twine to the edges of the panels, as illustrated in Fig. 5. Trim the pieces of twine so that they are all the same length—about 14 inches long.

Gather the ends of the twine together and tie them to a small nut. The perfect performance of your model parachute is going to depend upon having a suitable weight suspended from the lengths of twine.

Fold the parachute into its smallest size and loosely wind the twine about it. Throw the parachute as high into the air as possible. If it is correctly weighted, it will unfold and gracefully float to the ground. If more weight is needed, try screwing a small bolt into the nut. It is possible to add washers between the nut and bolt, should even more weight be required.

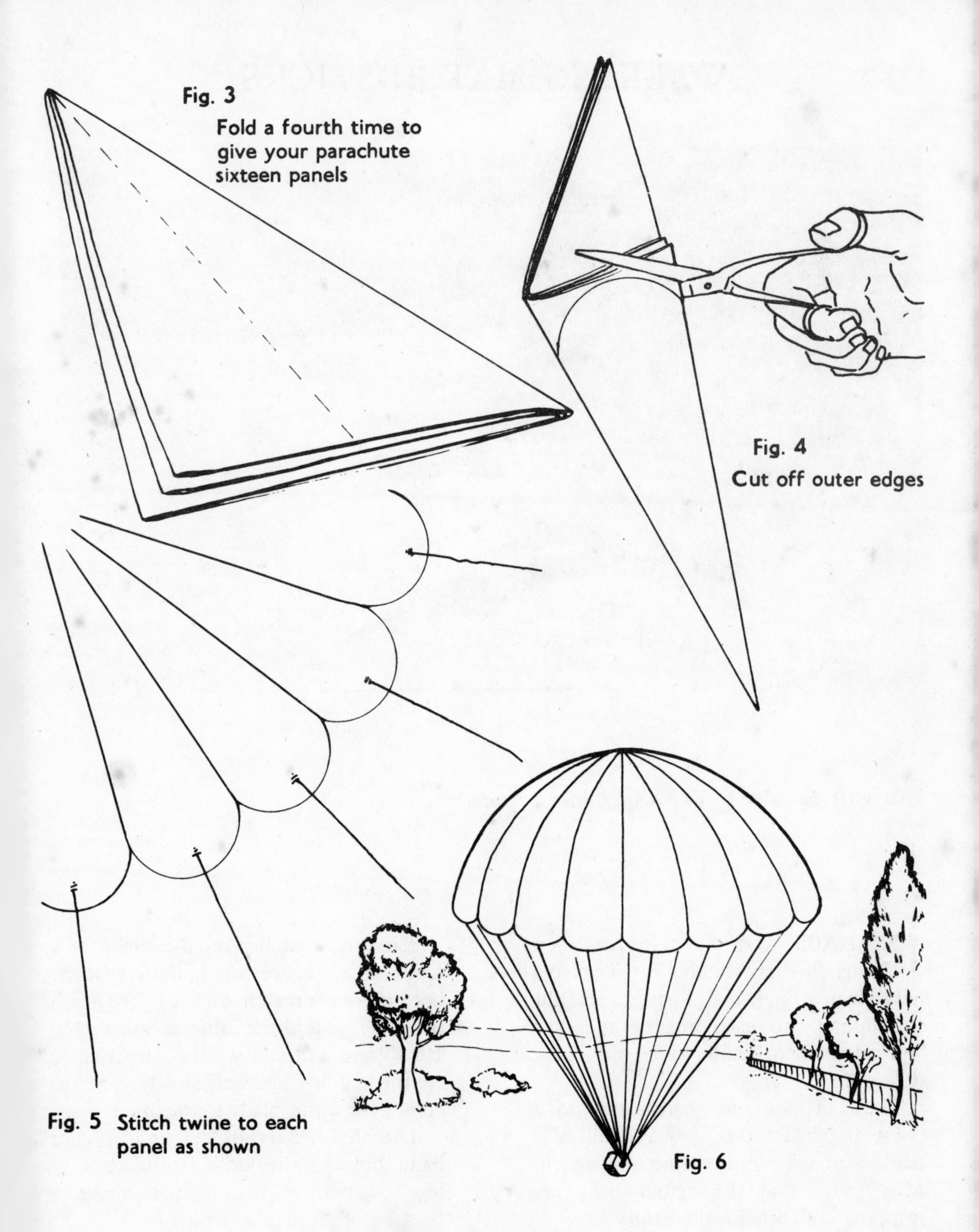
Fig. 3
Fold a fourth time to give your parachute sixteen panels
Fig. 4
Cut off outer edges
Fig. 5 Stitch twine to each panel as shown
Fig. 6

WALKING MATCH-STICKS

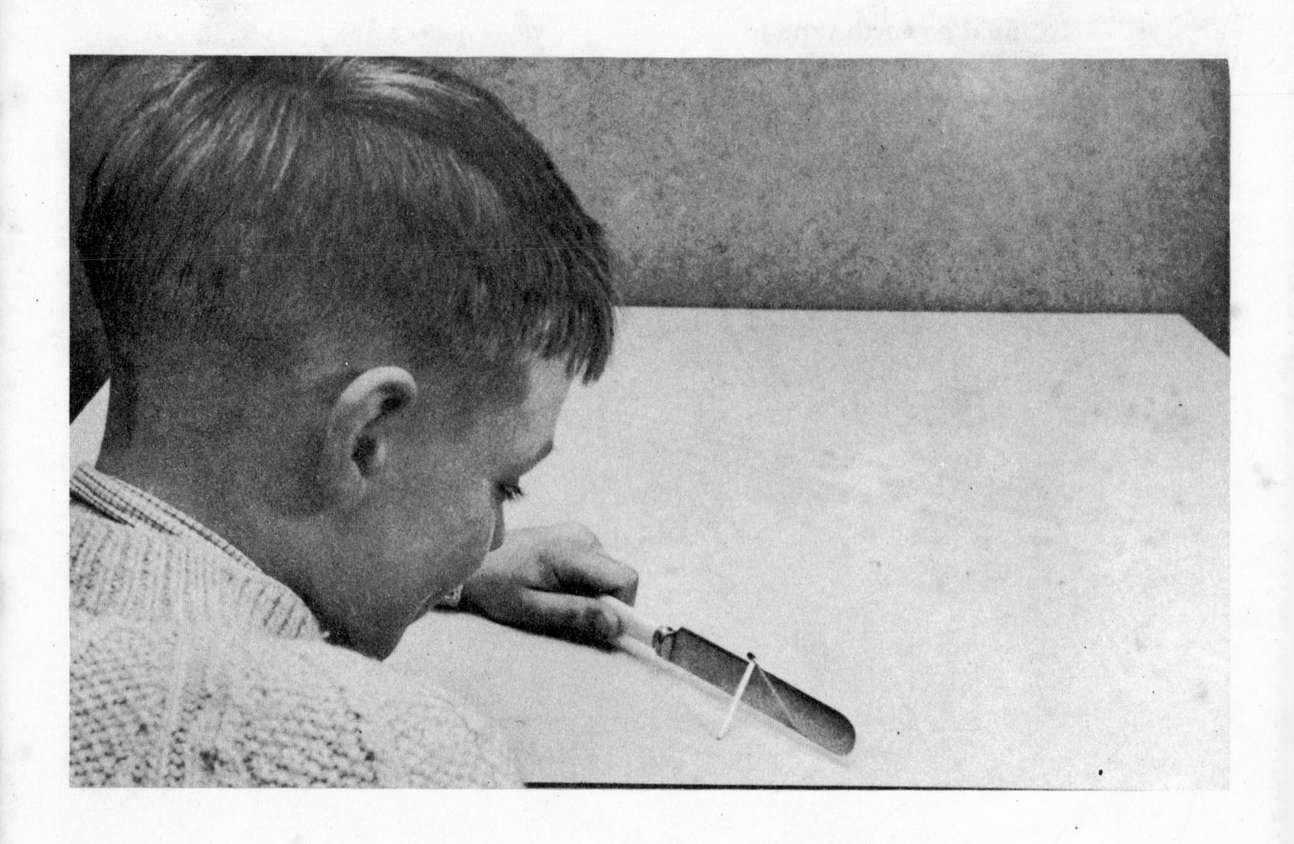

You will require : *Two match-sticks, knife.*

PERHAPS you have never seen a match-stick walking? We have never seen a single match-stick walk, but try joining two used matches together and watch them toddle along the blade of a knife.

First, sharpen one match-stalk to a point and insert this into a small split made near the top of the second match. Make sure that the match-sticks are gripping each other quite firmly.

Place the matches on the blade of a table-knife. Lower the knife so that the bottoms of the match-stick legs just touch the table. Hold the knife as still as you are able to and you will be surprised to see the match-sticks walk slowly from one end of the knife blade to the other.

The slight, nervous reaction of your hand holding the knife is sufficient to jog the pair of match-sticks along, a fraction of an inch at a time.

BLOW FOOTBALL

You will require : *Newspaper, gummed paper, wire, four match-boxes, table-tennis ball.*

WHEN it's raining outside and you are just longing for a game with a ball, why not try making a blow football game. Easily made in a matter of minutes, it can provide a great deal of fun.

Picture shows Pauline rolling newspaper into tubes about 8 inches in length. She used gummed paper to bind the two ends together and also put a band of gummed paper around the middle of each tube to lend additional strength.

The goals were made by bending two 12-inch pieces of wire into the shape of miniature goal-posts, and securing their ends in holes made in the middle of match-boxes.

An ordinary table-tennis ball serves as a football for this game of soccer. The illustration shows Pauline and Stephen with their game of blow football at full blast. Shortly after this photograph was taken, the referee warned both players that elbows on the table were not allowed, and that a free penalty blow would be awarded for any future infringement of this rule.

MAKING A LIFE MASK

You will require : *Plasticine, two drinking-straws, vaseline, plaster of Paris, brush.*

LIFE masks can be taken from a friend or relative. They will look like perfect examples of sculpture—true to the original in every way, even to skin texture.

Your model should wear a bathing-cap to protect the hair. He or she should then be seated in a low chair, his head resting comfortably upon the chair back, which may be padded for additional ease, and a towel wrapped closely around the neck.

Two lengths of drinking-straw, each about 4 inches long, should then be attached to the nostrils with plasticine, in such a way that the model experiences no difficulty in breathing with the mouth closed. (Fig. 1.)

Rub a coating of vaseline over the model's face—quite liberally over the closed eyes and lashes. This is to ensure that the plaster mould will lift free from his features with little effort.

Mix plaster of Paris with water until it is of a stiff, creamy consistency. Use a large spoon to apply the mixture to the model's features. Begin around the eyes and forehead, working downwards, quickly and easily, until the whole features are covered with a layer of plaster. Apply a second thick layer of plaster on top of the first, building up the mould until it is quite thick and strong. A brush can be used to smooth the final application. (Fig. 2.)

Allow ten minutes for the mould to set hard and then carefully lift it free from your model. You will find that the plaster has retained a perfect impression of the original features.

Brush the inside of the mould with a coating of soft soap or vaseline. (Fig. 3.) The complete inner surface should be covered in this manner, otherwise the casting will adhere to the mould and possibly mar the features.

Mix a further quantity of plaster and water. Pour this into the mould, filling it to the top, as shown in Fig. 4. While the plaster is still wet, a piece of bent wire or an opened paper-clip should be pressed into the plaster so that it may form a hanger.

Allow at least half an hour, possibly longer, for the plaster contents of the mould to dry out. Now lift the cast from the mould. With care, this can be achieved without having to break the mould, thus making it possible for further castings to be made.

With a small piece of cotton wool or soft cloth wipe the vaseline from the face of the life mask. This may then be painted or given a coating of clear varnish over the white plaster. Another novel method of finishing is to lightly brush a coating of coloured shoe polish over the face of the mask and then polish with a soft cloth.

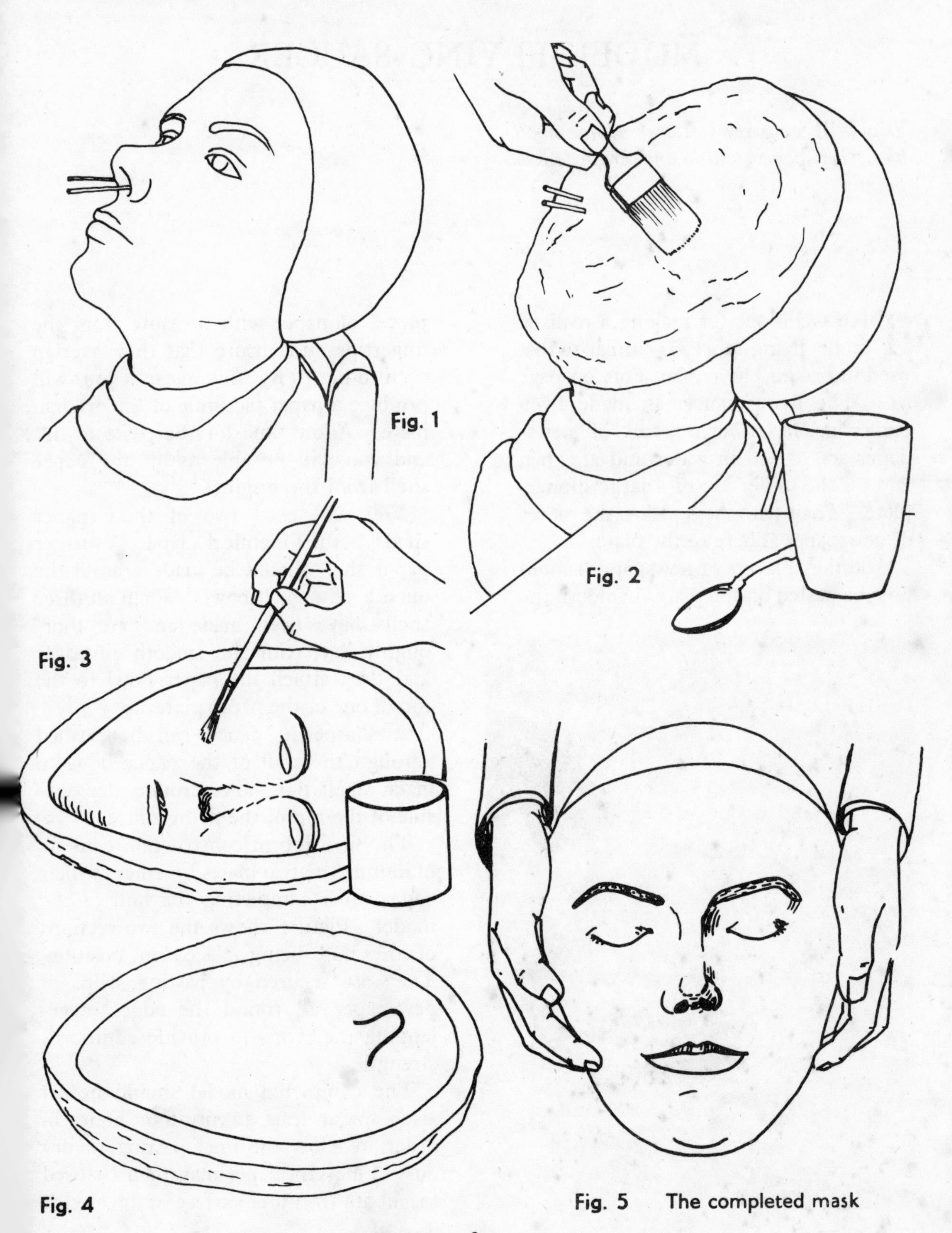

Fig. 1

Fig. 2

Fig. 3

Fig. 4

Fig. 5 The completed mask

MODEL FLYING-SAUCER

You will require : *Large plate, small bowl, newspaper, paste and brush, silver paint.*

THE technique for making a realistic model flying-saucer is similar to that used in making the trinket pots on page 94. The flying saucer is made from papier mâché. Torn pieces of newspaper are soaked in water and are then laid on the underside of a large dinner-plate. Their dampness makes the pieces of newspaper adhere to the plate.

Additional layers of newspaper should now be pasted on the plate. Smooth the pieces of paper with pressure from the fingertips and ensure that they overlap each other. By this means you will produce a paper facsimile of the original plate. Allow time for the paste to dry and you will be able to lift the paper shell from the original.

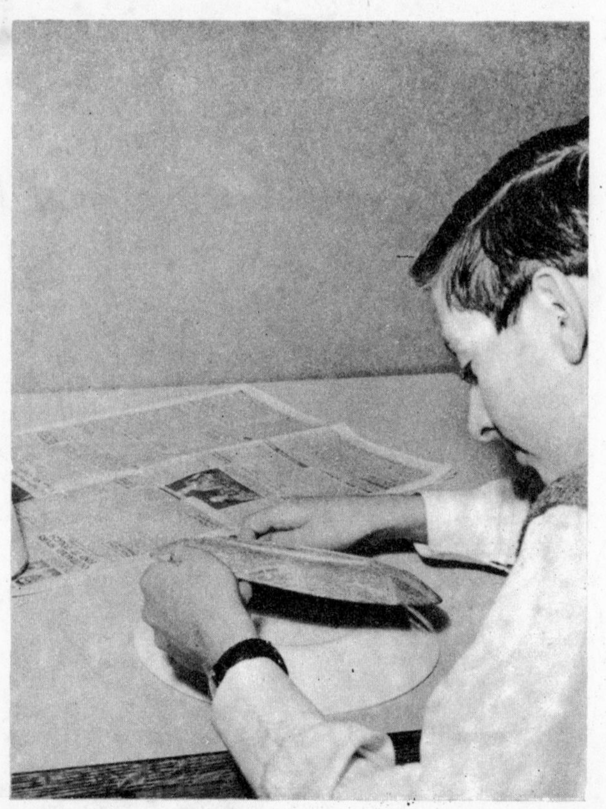

You will need two of these paper shells, both of identical shape. A further paper shell should be made around the outside of a small bowl. When all three shells have been made and are thoroughly dry, trim and smooth all edges and then attach the paper bowl to the top of one of the paper plates.

A sharpened pencil can be pushed through the wall of the paper bowl to make small port-holes around the outside of the top of the flying-saucer.

The final job of construction consists of joining the two plates together at their edges, thus completing the hull of the model. Picture shows the two sections of the hull being placed in position. They are secured by pasting strips of newspaper all round the edges, overlapping the strips to provide additional strength.

The completed model should be set aside for at least twenty-four hours in order to allow the final pasting to dry out. Fine sandpaper may then be used to smooth the outer surface of the model.

Your miniature flying-saucer is going to look best if finished in silver paint. Apply an undercoat of the paint, first stirring it well to ensure that the metalic powder is mixed. When dry, it may be necessary to sandpaper where any bad inequalities of the surface have shown up. A second application of the paint should be all that is then required.

Your finished model is going to look most realistic if it is allowed to hang from the ceiling in a corner of your room. Use a fine white thread with which to suspend your model. It will be hard to detect from the ceiling, itself, at a distance, and your miniature flying-saucer will have every appearance of being in flight.

LUCKY MASCOTS

You will require : *Cardboard, scissors, pencil, tracing-paper, scraps of felt, lace and fabrics, glue.*

IT is a comparatively easy matter to make gay little lucky mascots. They can be used as wall decorations, party favours or, in smaller editions, as unusual brooches and lapel pins.

First, you will need a suitable cardboard foundation on which to make your mascot. The simple outline drawings will provide suitable foundations for a golliwog and a clown mascot. Place a sheet of tracing-paper on one or the other outline, draw round it, and then transfer this outline to a sheet of cardboard.

Cut the cardboard shape out and then choose appropriate pieces of coloured felt and fabric for the various parts of the mascot's costume.

For instance, the golliwog has bright yellow trousers, a scarlet jacket, a blue waistcoat with scarlet buttons and, of course, a black face with large eyes of white and black felt.

Having chosen a piece of fabric for a certain part of the costume, place the cardboard cut-out on the cloth and draw round it with pencil or piece of sharpened chalk. Allow a good margin all round and then cut to shape. Use a good-quality tube glue to stick the fabric to the card, turning the margin of cloth down and glueing it securely to the back of the mascot. Repeat until your mascot is fully clothed.

THE THOUGHT READER

You will require : *About two-dozen assorted articles.*

PAULINE put on her gipsy-girl costume again to try out this thought-reading trick on Robert. She had to take young Stephen into her confidence, but the trick was so easy that he had no trouble in helping her to thoroughly mystify Robert—and several adults who were also present.

Having arranged a number of small articles on the table she told Robert that she would go out of the room while he pointed to the article that he was thinking of. There was no need for him to speak. She could read his thoughts. When she returned to the room, even Stephen did not speak to her. He simply pointed to article after article until she suddenly stopped him—and she never failed to stop just as his finger was pointing to the very article that Robert had pointed to when she had been out of the room.

In the end she told Robert how it had been possible for her to find out which article he had had in mind. On the table there were two articles (both watches, as it happened) that had leather on them. She had arranged with Stephen that, immediately before pointing to the article singled out by Robert, he would first point to one or other of the leather articles. She then knew that the next thing that Stephen pointed to would be the correct one.

Even when Robert pointed to one of the watches this worked. Stephen pointed first to the other watch and then to the one that Robert had chosen.

TRINKET POT

You will require : *Jam-jar, newspaper, paste, cardboard, scissors, paints and brush.*

THESE useful little trinket pots are simple enough to make, and certainly do not require any expensive materials. When completed they are handy receptacles for studs, buttons, tie-pins, jewellery, etc.

Tear an old newspaper into small scraps and soak a few of these in a saucer of water. Use these damp pieces of newspaper to cover the bottom part of a jam-jar. Because they are wet you will find that the paper will stick to the glass surface.

Now apply further layers of paper, by pasting them to each preceding layer. Overlap the pieces of paper and make quite sure that each layer completely

Fig. 1

Fig. 2

Tabs of handle turned down

Under side of lid with card flange in position

Card flange $\frac{1}{4}$", $\frac{1}{2}$", 12"

Side view of lid showing flange and handle

covers the first before adding another. Figure 1 shows how your trinket pot looks in the beginning.

When you have built the layers of paper up to a good thickness, the work must be put on one side to dry out. This may need at least twenty-four hours in a warm room. When dry, the paper shell may be lifted free from the end of the jar. If you have made it well it will be found to be light but strong.

At this stage make sure that the rim of your pot is smooth. Paste further strips of paper over the edge, overlapping each piece as you work round the pot, until the rim is completely reinforced. Stick down any loose paper there may be on the inside or outside of the pot. If greater strength is required, additional layers of paper may be pasted around the sides.

The lid of the pot is cut from a piece of thick cardboard. Cut a circle of cardboard that is about ½ inch larger in diameter than the mouth of the pot. From a thinner piece of card cut a strip measuring 12 inches long by ¾ inch wide. Fold this down the centre so that there is ¼ inch on one side of the fold and ½ inch on the other. With straight cuts of the scissors remove triangular pieces of card from the ½-inch side, as shown in Fig. 2.

This thinner card flange is then bent round so that it fits quite easily into the mouth of the pot. Glue the overlapping ends of the flange together to fix this size, then bend the small triangular tabs under, and glue them to the underside of the lid.

Pass the two ends of a thin strip of card through a hole in the centre of the lid and glue these down to the underside of the lid. This will provide a base for a handle.

Above pictures show the pot and lid, at this stage. One or two layers of pasted paper should be added to the top and sides of the lid to strengthen it, and more paper should be pasted around the foundation of the handle.

All that remains is to paint the lid and pot as attractively as possible. The inside is best painted white or cream. Choose gay colours for the outside. Try to use a matching pattern for the lid. A coat of clear varnish will preserve your colours.

THE BOOK RACE

You will require : *Books and competitors.*

NOT one of the fastest race games for a party or family gathering, but certainly one of the funniest, is the " book race."

The rules are quite simple. You can have as many competitors as the course will hold. Each runner is given a book which must be placed on the head before the start of the race, and which must still be balancing there in position when the finishing-line is crossed. Anyone who loses their book during the race must return to the beginning and start all over again.

On no account must the book be held in position during the course of the race.

If competitors are agreeable, handicapping may either be made by distance or by giving better performers a heavier volume to transport.

As you can see by this illustration, the " gang " are thoroughly enjoying this race, with Baby Andrew way out in front —er—is someone cheating there ?

PUBLISHED BY ASSOCIATED NEWSPAPERS LTD., LONDON, E.C.4 AND
PRINTED IN GREAT BRITAIN BY MORRISON AND GIBB LTD., LONDON AND EDINBURGH